ADVERTISING

ADVERTISING
New Techniques for Visual Seduction

Uwe Stoklossa / Edited by Thomas Rempen

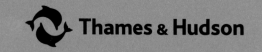

Everything that can be written about creativity has already been written in this field where, as in no other, there is a constant, frantic search for new texts and images that will arouse the interest and appetites of millions of people. But maybe there is still something we can add.

The 'secret seducers' are what we sometimes call the visual wizards that work in ad agencies, only the public already knows that the seduction is not secret at all; the ideas are developed consciously and artistically with a view to earning a tiny, inaudible, intimate and admiring round of applause.

This is the art which can make advertising so enjoyable, attractive, and successful. Sometimes it's just words that make us feel cheerful, alert or curious, and sometimes it's pictures, or it can even be the inexplicable dynamism of word and picture combined, forming a context that takes us by surprise. And sometimes it's strange and mysterious images, optical illusions – eye-fooling, don't-believe-it images that grab the

attention, gnaw through to the brain, and jangle the nerve-ends: you catch your breath, you're irritated, you stop in mid-sentence…something's wrong. There's a puzzle here that needs to be solved.

It's the second glance that solves the riddle, and the solution relieves and releases us, leaving us cheerful, relaxed, and pleased with ourselves. Images that can do that are magical – the tricks of the ad trade.

Those who invent these tricks are the great wizards and seducers in the world of communications. They are artists who know the secrets that are hidden from the rest of us – hidden, that is, until now. But now these visual tricks have been collected – they are all set out and explained in the first section of this book, like specimens in a glass case. Then, in the second section, the author describes to us how the world of visual perception works, and how its special qualities can be put to effective use.

This is the first book to explain how to catch the eye-catching, how to make perception perceivable, how to focus on focus. Thanks to this book, you can study all the tricks for yourself.

The curator of this exhibition is a young man named Uwe Stoklossa, who as a student of mine expressed his displeasure at having to think up new ideas without being able to study how they came into being. The conglomeration of texts which scientifically and long-windedly sought to explain the mechanisms of vision were not enough for his purposes: he needed visual aids.

I was not, therefore, surprised when two years ago he came to me with a pile of books and a subject for a dissertation which, with its scientific bias, was somewhat unusual for a student taking a degree in communications design: 'Phenomena of Perception'.

Uwe wanted to take a new look at these mysteries, and that is precisely what he has done. And with the diligence and acuity of a Sherlock Holmes, he has examined every clue. The dissertation grew into a veritable thesis, with the title: 'I See Nothing That You Can't See', and by the time it was

finished, it was so fascinating and so illuminating that I could not resist showing it to the publisher Hermann Schmidt.

The rest of this labour of love took one and a half years. Uwe Stoklossa went on searching, collecting, analysing, dissecting, adding, checking, selecting and arranging.

All the examples come from the highly competitive world of advertising, because here more than anywhere else, designers are expected to work their magic in order not only to create the right image for the product, but also to ensure that this image will be new, striking, surprising, and different from all the others.

This collection provides a unique compendium. You can skim, browse or bury yourself in it. You can study it. And it will become a must for art directors, who spend their lives on the look-out for new ideas, new tricks. We hope it will lead to an even greater use of the irresistible creative energy that goes together with such (literally) unbelievable ideas and images. The wide variety

of examples in each category shows how much has already been achieved, but it also implies an unlimited potential for growth in the future.

As we all know, the eye comes before the brain. Have fun, though, with both of them.

Thomas Rempen
Düsseldorf and Essen, July 2005

SEEING AND BEING SEEN

Imagine you're in any agency in any country, preparing a campaign for any product made by any customer. As always, the presentation has to be ready for tomorrow, and the art director and his colleagues are just having a look at what the creative team has come up with.

As often happens, the ideas aren't bad, but then come the announcements that wreck all hope of an early finish, and send all the proposals sliding off into the wide blue yonder of the advertising world's infinite possibilities: 'It doesn't really grab you.' 'There's nothing that actually holds your attention.' 'Where's the eye-catcher?' Not to mention the one that advertisers have made all their own, and is tantamount to a definitive no: 'We've seen it all before.'

That's the pronouncement that tells you everything about the ad world and its greatest problem. Ads fight a fierce battle every day against countless competitors just to grab a few seconds of people's attention. The competition doesn't consist just of other ads; also out there in the arena are the magazine articles, the traffic, the manly hunk or the gorgeous girl that happens to be passing by, the hooting car, the radio, the TV...

If a design is to grab people's attention, it must offer something really extraordinary – and sometimes it does. But only when the sense of sight, which is extremely demanding and thoroughly spoilt for choice, is confronted with something that is not 'any old thing' or 'seen it before'. And that brings us back to the problem our agency is facing the day before the presentation. Because having to (and wanting to) come up with something new all the time is not always easy amid the everyday stress of agency life and the ever-present danger of falling into a rut.

It was this situation that gave rise to the idea of the book you are now holding. It is an attempt to answer the question: 'Are there any rules to tell you when the blink of an eye turns into a feast for the eye? Why do we sometimes like to take a second look, and sometimes only want to look away?'

These questions could only be answered by examining thousands and thousands of ads for precisely this information. The 'winners' that passed the test then had to be studied to determine their common features, and sorted into categories. And lo and behold, it really is possible to discover systems, methods, shared features and, ultimately, a phenomenology of visual seduction.

This is what you will find in the first part of the book. There are ten clear categories, for your enjoyment, inspiration and admiration, and they make up an exhibition of the finest ideas from the best creative teams in the world when it comes to visual seduction. Each 'exhibit' is worth a second look, and should also stimulate some creative thoughts of your own.

But creatives are curious, and when the first effects of a trick have worn off, we want to know more. It's like watching a magician: the magic itself is not enough – we want to know how it's done. How and why did the trick work? Fortunately, in this context the experts are the exact opposite of magicians, because they are only too pleased to reveal and explain all. That is how the second part of this book came into being. It is a look behind the scenes of the magic show.

From the standpoint of the different disciplines of science and art, all the phenomena related to sight and seeing are explained as far as possible in the light of present-day knowledge. For close observation makes one thing very clear: in spite of long and painstaking research in all the different disciplines, there are still many blind spots when it comes to describing and explaining visual

perception. Perhaps, though, that is why the field is such an exciting one to explore.

Despite the large number of examples, this book should not give anyone the feeling that everything has now been done. Quite the contrary. The systematic classification of these examples is designed to provide you with a kind of handbook of visual seduction, which you can use as a starting-point for a whole host of startling new concepts.

On some pages, I have deliberately put together examples that are very similar in character. This is in no way meant as a criticism implying that the designers copied one another; it simply shows that the same creative methods can be used in lots of different ways, each one of which can be stunning and even award-winning in its own category.

Just think how many films are made that tell the story of a man and woman who meet, can't stand each other at first, and then after a catalogue of blunders and misunderstandings, finally fall in love. Even though the formula is old and hackneyed, it can still make us have a good cry, or a good laugh, and might even go on to win an Oscar. But of course it has to be brilliantly made.

Against this background, I hope all the readers and users of this book will derive Oscar-winning ideas, encouragement, and success with whatever tricks they discover or invent. Above all, though, I hope you will have a lot of fun as you delve into the most fascinating of all our senses: sight.

Uwe Stoklossa

CONTENTS

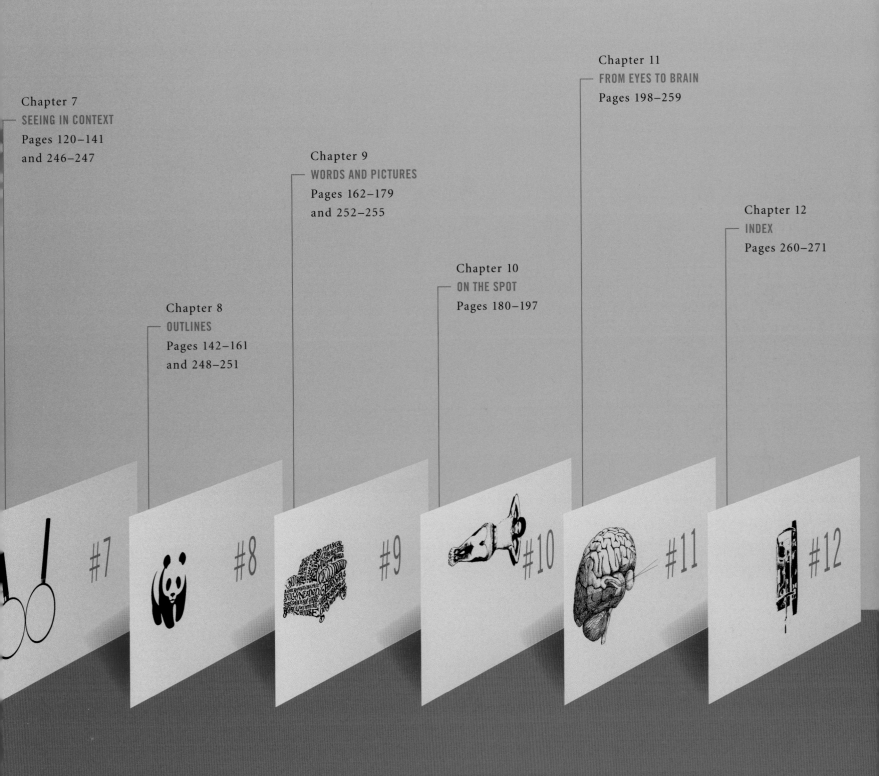

#7   #8   #9   #10   #11   #12

The eyes deliver a
continuous stream
of data that passes
unfiltered to the brain.
The visual centres of
our brains then have to
decide which pieces of
information constitute
the figure and which
the background. The
apparent chaos of the
visual raw data is put
into meaningful order

#1 FIGURE AND GROUND

by this process. The first
and most important
question, then, is what
should be perceived as
the subject, and what as
the formless ground. The
answer doesn't always
have to be clear, because
there is no such thing
as right or wrong in
many cases. Sometimes
different interpretations
will simply lead to
different solutions.

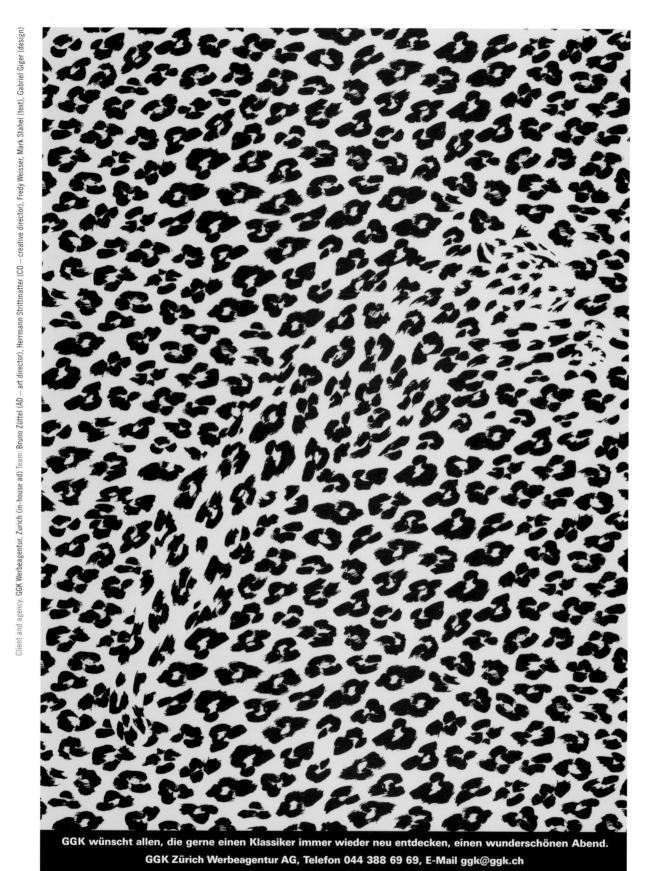

GGK wünscht allen, die gerne einen Klassiker immer wieder neu entdecken, einen wunderschönen Abend.

GGK Zürich Werbeagentur AG, Telefon 044 388 69 69, E-Mail ggk@ggk.ch

A Swiss ad agency's own ad in the programme of the Locarno Film Festival 2005 (founded in 1947), for which the top award is The Golden Leopard. The text below reads: 'GGK wishes a wonderful evening to all who like to go on rediscovering a classic.'

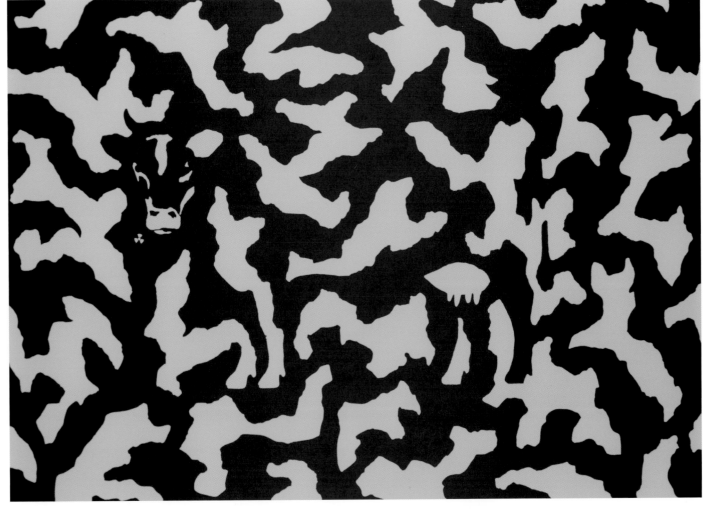

Poster from the
Non-Poster series IQ
against radioactive
pollution, after the
Chernobyl disaster
of 1986.

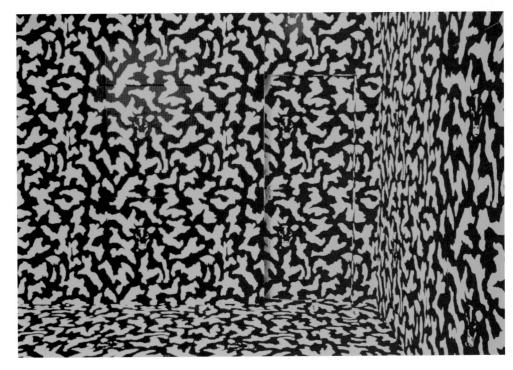

The same motif as an
installation in the Von-
der-Heydt Museum in
Wuppertal.

'It's not just the rainforest that's dying. You can protect the last rainforests on our planet. Give online at: www.wwf.de.'

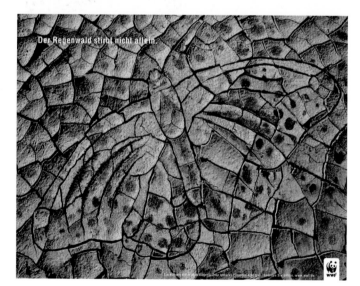

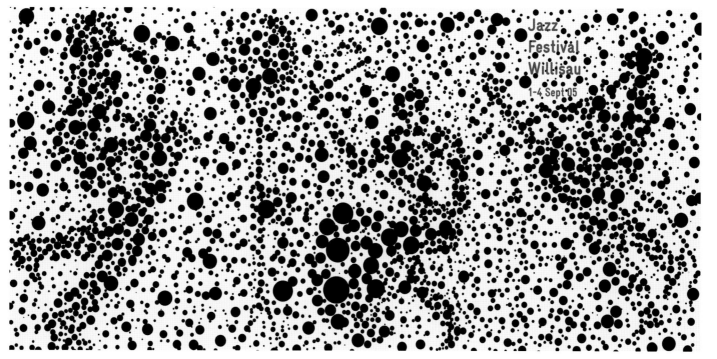

Cover of a book on the history of office chairs.

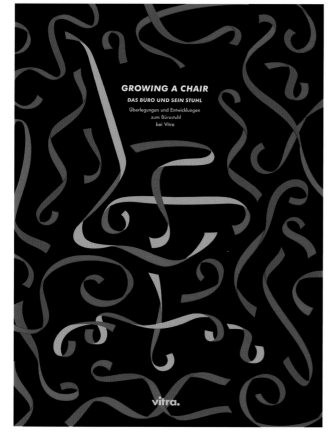

The São Paulo biennial
art festival: 'Art and
you, two as one.'

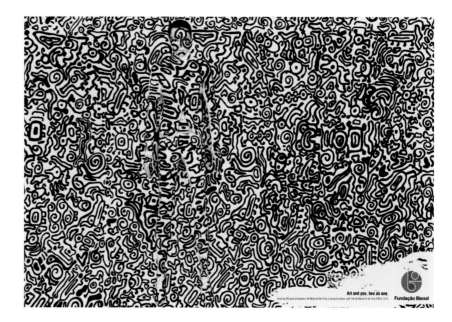

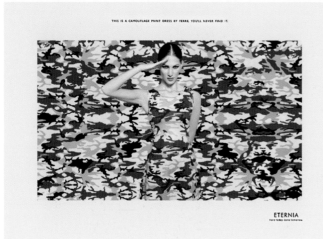

Shop for exclusive
designer wear:
'You'll never find it.'

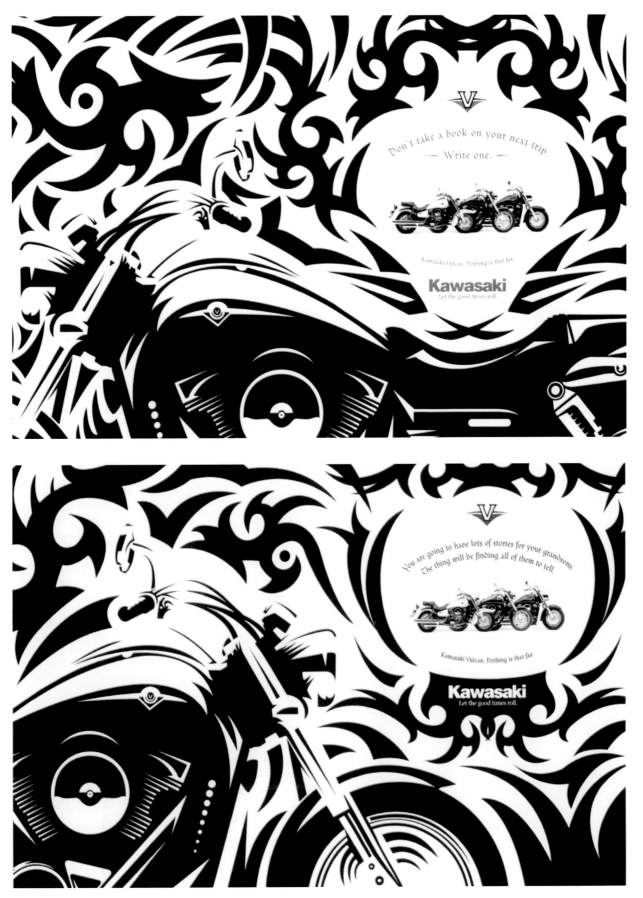

Client: Singapore Prevention of Cruelty to Animals Agency: Leo Burnett, Singapore AD: Koh Hwee Peng, Tay Guan Hin Photo: Alex Kaikeong

Lost and found
service of an animal
protection society in
Singapore.

Client: Swatch Agency: Neogama/BBH, São Paulo AD: Sidney Araujo

A range of transparent
watches by Swatch.
'Fashions change.
It adapts.'

Advertising advertises
itself with individual
posters. 'Advertising
makes the everyday
less grey.'

Outdoor advertising by a
print shop, with posters
designed to blend in
with the surroundings:
'We just love to print.'

This ad for army
vehicles exaggerates
the idea of camouflage.
You can't see a vehicle
anywhere in the picture.

The outline of a
glass of Carlsberg
can be seen in the
negative space.

Below, a caricature of
Sigmund Freud; left,
an adaptation for a
Gay Festival in Oslo.

WHAT'S ON A MAN'S MIND

gay days

Oslo gay festival june 13 - 22

Poster for the opera
Don Giovanni. The
lead character is
an unscrupulous
womanizer, whose lust
costs him his life.

THE IMPACT
OF THE HOLOCAUST AND GENOCIDE
ON JEWS & CHRISTIANS

**Remembering
for
the Future**

An International Scholars' Conference,
Oxford, 10–13 July 1988
Public Conference,
London 15 July 1988

Exhibition of work by
Shigeo Fukuda.

Client: Merry Down Agency: Campbell Doyle Dye, London Illustration: Giles Revell (top left), Greg Clarke (top right), Martin Haake (below left), Mark Denton (below right)

Cover of magazine
Merry Down, which
always presents
different images
upside down
or downside up.

Client: Hong Kong Bank Agency: Euro RSCG Ball, Singapore AD: Michael Tan

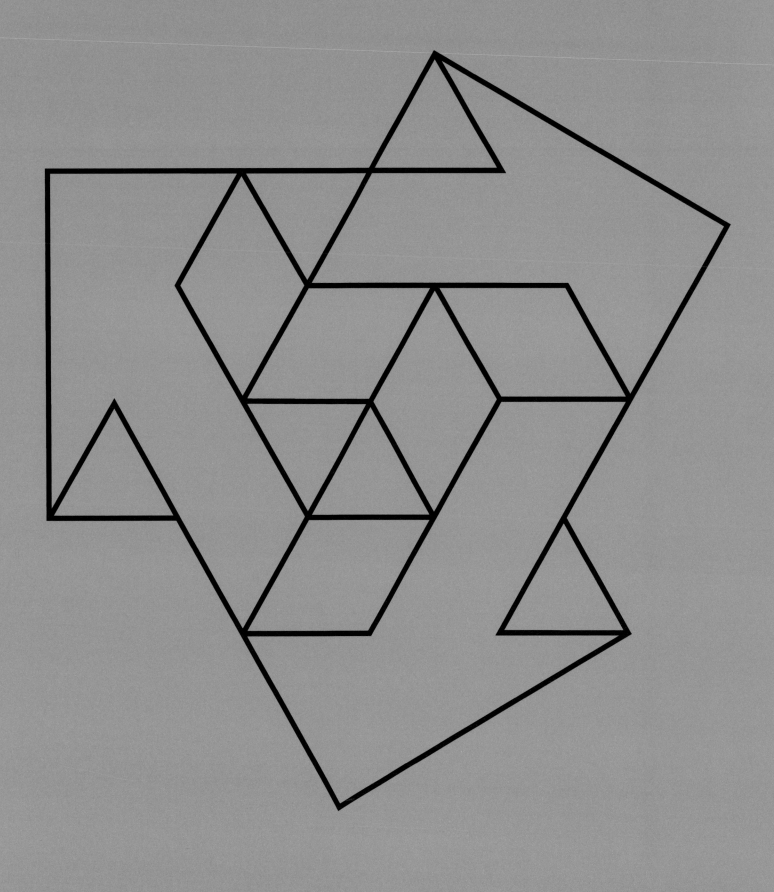

The major handicap
with our sight is that
we always have to find
our way round a three-
dimensional world,
but can only see in two
dimensions. The image
that is projected through
the lens to the rear of the
eye onto the retina is just
as flat as a photograph.
Therefore there is no
direct information about
spatial depth. This has
to be painstakingly
constructed through

#2 TWO AND THREE DIMENSIONS

hidden clues such as light
and shade, overlapping,
and various other factors
derived from learning
or experience. Because
of this weakness, the
observer can easily be
misled. Many of the
following examples
exploit the fact that a
well-constructed two-
dimensional image can
be extremely difficult to
distinguish from three-
dimensional reality.

Client: Martini Agency: McCann-Erickson, Paris AD: Vincent D'Amiens

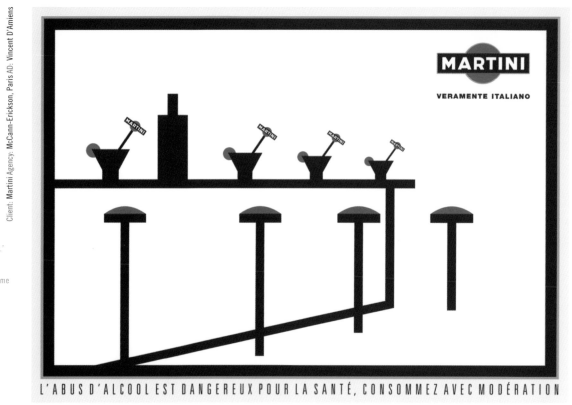

'Martini. Truly Italian.'

'Alcohol abuse is a health hazard. Consume with moderation.'

In a commercial for a Mercedes convertible, the two-dimensional representation of a sound pattern is made to depict a drive through a three-dimensional landscape. 'Hear the summer in a Mercedes Benz convertible'

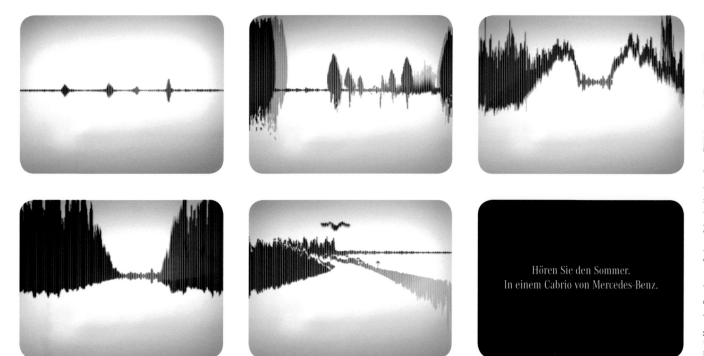

Hören Sie den Sommer.
In einem Cabrio von Mercedes-Benz.

Client: Mercedes-Benz Agency: Springer & Jacoby, Hamburg Team: Till Hohmann, Axel Thomsen (CD), Justus von Engelhardt, Tobias Gradert-Hinzpeter (AD), Florian Kähler, Florian Pagel (copy)

Client: Raumtechnik Messebau & Event Services GmbH Agency: GPP Werbeagentur, Stuttgart AD: Michael Preiswerk

A firm specializing
in exhibition spaces
printed drawings on
its equipment that
both inspire and
confuse.

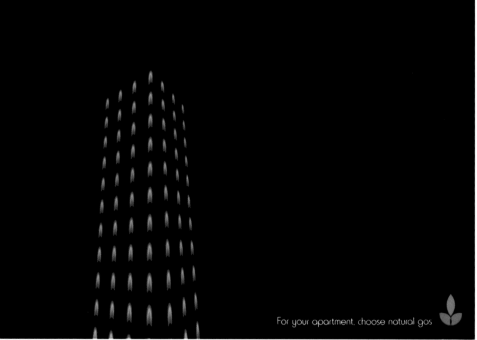

Client: Natural Gas Company Agency: Duval Guillaume, Brussels AD: Alain Janssens

For your apartment, choose natural gas

The arrangement of
the individual flames
creates a powerful
spatial effect.

TWO AND THREE DIMENSIONS   29

In logo design, three-dimensional effects are a very popular stylistic device.

2

1

4

3

6

5

7

8

9

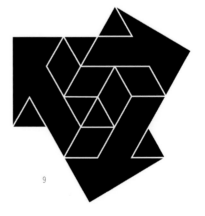

1: Bank: Banca Del Monte Di Parma, Italy 2: Construction industry: Multicon, USA 3: Food industry: La Torre Conserves, Mexico 4: Bank: Phildrew Ventures, UK 5: Mobile network: Naray International Telecommunications, Korea 6: Construction company: TeaYoung Construction, Korea 7: Contact lens company: Occulenti, Netherlands 8: Organization for Korea Atomic Energy Awareness (OKAEA), Korea 9: Design agency: Visual Syntax Design, USA

10: Radio station: Dimension, USA 11: Steel industry: Tasaki Steel Co., Japan 12: Film: Magic Hour Pictures, Korea
13: Insurance: Hanil Life Insurance, Korea 14: Finance: Korea Venture Capital Association, Korea 15: Petroleum: Total, France
16: Paint: Fuller Paints, USA 17: Hotel: Paradise Hotel, Korea 18: TV station: Korea Satellite Communications, Korea

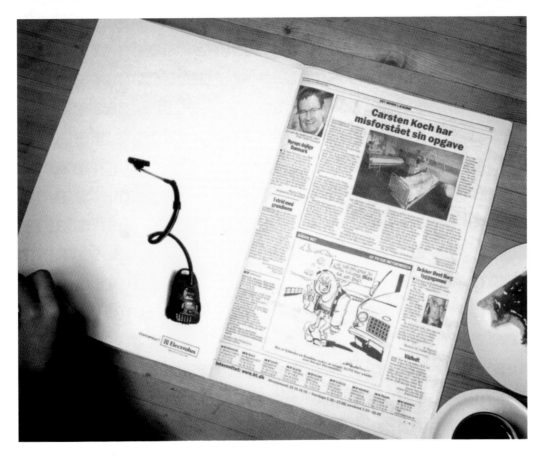

Two-page ad. At first sight, it seems as if the right-hand page is being sucked in from behind. The ad for a vacuum cleaner on the following page explains why.

Client: Deutsche Telekom Agency: Springer & Jacoby Werbung, Hamburg AD: Uta Jugert, Rolf Leger, Alexander Sehrbrock, Nina Rühmkorf

'Wind and weather direct to your mobile phone.'

During the restoration of the Brandenburg Gate in Berlin, German Telecom was allowed to use it for advertising, so that it would not disappear altogether from public view. Above: 'We bring people together.' Below: 'Love each other.'

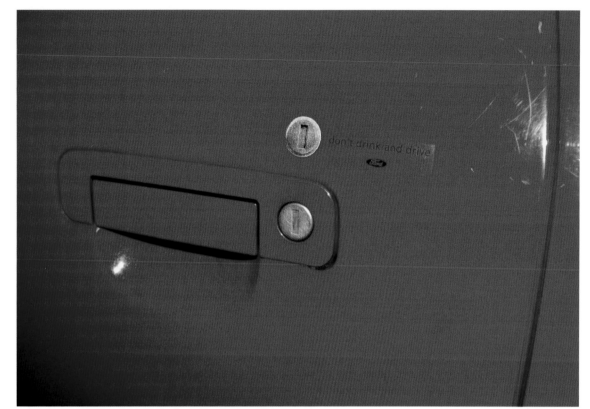

Two stickers with aptly placed warnings.

In a competition held
in conjunction with the
Universität der Künste in
Berlin, the slogan of the
Bayerische Immobilien
Gruppe, 'Buildings
with Faces', had to be
graphically illustrated.

This windscreen shade depicts a hugely exaggerated car interior, showing how much room there is in the little Smart.

Car design by a discount engineering firm: 'We can't afford a van like this. No wonder, at our prices.'

Client: DaimlerChrysler AG Agency: Scholz & Friends, Berlin AD: Sandra Schilling

'No more clutch. With the
new 6-gear automatic in the
Sprinter. Test the SprintShift.'

Client: Viventy Agency: Springer & Jacoby Werbung, Hamburg AD: Anke Peters

'Try it on!' The three-dimensional
can be taken for two-dimensional.
These are real jackets. When they
are 'removed', a text explains the
offer and identifies the chainstore.

This chapter also deals with perception of space. Here, however, the observer is not deceived but is invited, by means of a staged scene, to see more than is actually necessary. The spatial arrangement and positioning of the elements of the picture are basically clear.

#3 FOREGROUND AND BACKGROUND

However, the camera's standpoint is so precise, and the staging of the scene so skilful, that the observer is forced to establish a connection between the foreground and background. In this way, the designer removes the spatial gap between the two.

faire du ciel le plus bel endroit de la terre

AIR FRANCE

Air France has been using the same visual trick for many years, though with different scenes, in order to illustrate the connection between near and far. The slogan reads: 'Make the sky the loveliest place on Earth.'

'New Business Class with reclining seats.'

Client: Samsung Agency: Cheil Communications America, Irvine, CA AD: lovemando, Wendy Vinzant Photo: Michael Schnabel

Club holidays for
young adults. The
staged 'spontaneity'
of the scene creates
a number of visual
double entendres.

A competition held by the City of Paris: 'Cleanliness, energy, travel, recycling, noise. Environmental grants. Turn what's in your head into reality.'

Client: **Shell Select (not used)** Agency: **JWT, Hamburg** AD: **Esther Lauth, Gitte Reckord**

An unused idea from
a series designed
to introduce
Shell's Select Shops.

Commission: **Kreativschule** final project on the subject of the Catholic Church Team: Florian Bachofen, Nicole Domokos, Andrea Dübendorfer (AD), David Hugentobler (copy) Photo: Alfonso Smith

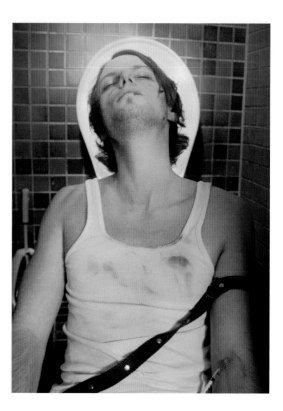

'Jesus was human too.'
Ads for the Catholic Church

Haloes on tram windows –
heaven-sent inspiration?

More haloes,
on the windows
of a tram stop.

Client: Pfizer, Nicorette Agency: BMP DDB, London AD: Ed Morris

Two campaigns for products
to stop people smoking.

Client: Pfizer, Nicorette Agency: Colenso BBDO, Auckland AD: Quentin Pfiszter, Leo Premutico Photo: Julian Wolkenstein

'The Class A Mercedes.
There's plenty of space
hidden inside.'

'The Class A Mercedes
has extraordinarily
solid road-holding.'

'For the Class A
Mercedes, the road is
a no-smoking area.'

'Nothing helps you
keep your car closer
than LoJack.'

'With LoJack you
are in control of
your car's safety.'

Audi TT. Nice stuff.

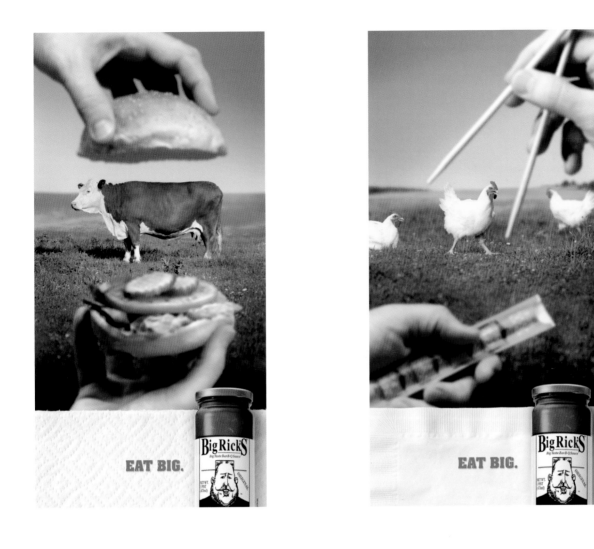

Client: Matchbox Agency: Jung von Matt, Hamburg AD: Joachim Silber Photo: Gulliver Theis, Philip Toledano, Kai Wiechmann, Ivo von Renner

Client: Vileda Agency: Leo Burnett, Lisbon AD: Vera Machado Photo: Francisco Prata

Our visual system not only figures out the contours, shapes and views of things, but also their sizes. Human beings have a well-trained and highly developed sense of the natural size and proportions of objects and people. That is why

#4 BIG AND SMALL

it comes as a shock and therefore immediately grabs the attention when different items in a scene are out of proportion to each other. The ads in the following chapter make use of this potential for deliberate provocation.

Client: Weru Agency: Scholz & Friends, Berlin AD: Kay Luebke Photo: Ralph Baiker

Advertising campaign for
soundproof windows.

Client: Kookai Agency: CLM/BBDO, Issy-les-Moulineaux AD: Christhophe Dru Photo: Les Guzman

Designer label for
women only.

Client: F&N Coca-Cola Agency: Bates Asia, Kuala Lumpur AD: Mike Chin Photo: Khoo Choo Kian

600 km mega-marathon
in Kuala Lumpur.

Client: Pilena Agency: Tiempo BBDO, Barcelona AD: Gabriel Penalva Photo: Ramón Serrano

Anti-dandruff
shampoo.

1.04 acres of the world's rainforests disappear every second. Stop the destruction now. To see how you can help the WWF, visit us at www.panda.org today.

Ads for a festival
of short films.

Internet provider with particularly
fast data flow ('ten times faster
than ISDN').

Left: Diet Pepsi.

Below: Yoghurt drink
with 0.1% fat.

Nur 0,1% Fett.

Fear and Arrogance—Enemies of Peace.

Client: Greenpeace Agency: Mukai & Associates, Tokyo AD: Hideo Mukai Photo: Eiichiro Sakata

Client: Wasa Agency: Bates Red Cell, Oslo AD: Jack Hagbru

Wasabrød er rikt på fiber fordi det er bakt av hele kornet waša

'Full of roughage because it's
baked from wholemeal flour.'

Client: Laforet Agency: Dentsu, Tokyo AD: Yuji Tokuda Photo: Hatsuhiko Okada

actual size

actual size

Model cars that are
true to the original.

Client: Duxbury Dollhouse Agency: Hill Holliday, Boston Team: Kevin Daley (AD), Rick McHugh (copy) Photo: Guido Vitti

THE DUXBURY DOLLHOUSE
REALLY AUTHENTIC MINIATURES 781.837.1195

THE DUXBURY DOLLHOUSE
REALLY AUTHENTIC MINIATURES 781.837.1195

Window display for the jeweller H. Stern. Items of jewelry are used as interior decoration.

Client: Juwelier H. Stern (designed in-house)

This chapter shows that the sense of sight is capable of multitasking. Here, objects are perceived as they are, but at the same time, because of the way they have been arranged, they show us something new and transcendent. The reason for this is to be found in the brain's extraordinary capacity for abstraction.

#5 COMPOSITIONS

So long as the outer form of a familiar object is recognizable, it doesn't seem to matter what individual parts it is composed of. The size and arrangement of these parts can be organized in such a way that the observer is made to see the whole object first and its components second, or vice versa.

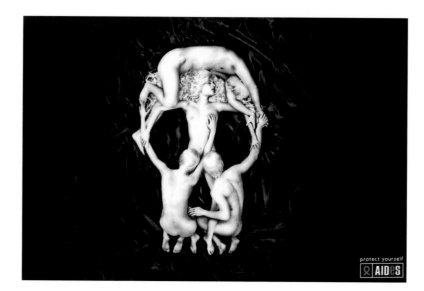

Client: **Vizir** Agency: **Leo Burnett, Warsaw** AD: **Martin Winther** Photo: **Sebastian Hanel**

ERGONOMISCH SITZEN.

DAUPHIN
HumanDesign® Company

Manufacturers
of ergonomic
office furniture.

Client: Dauphin GmbH & Co. Agency: Q Werbeagentur AG, Munich AD: Katharina Heitkamm Photo: Sonja Mueller

Client: Runners Point Agency: Jung von Matt, Hamburg AD: Martin Terhart, Philipp Cerne

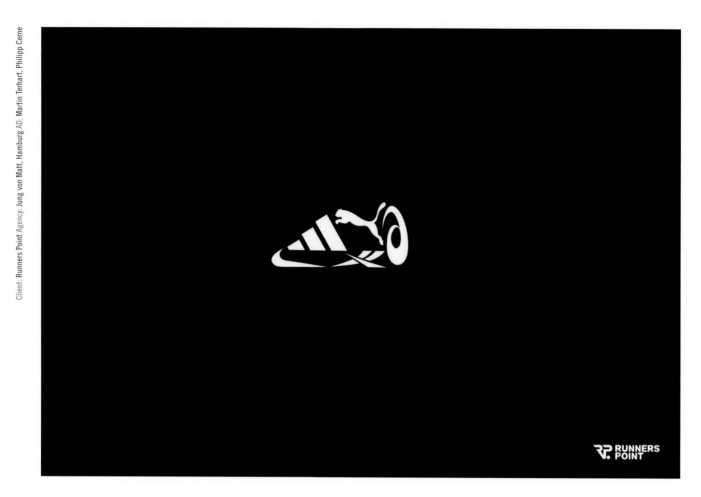

Visual variations on the Audi slogan 'Vorsprung durch Technik'.

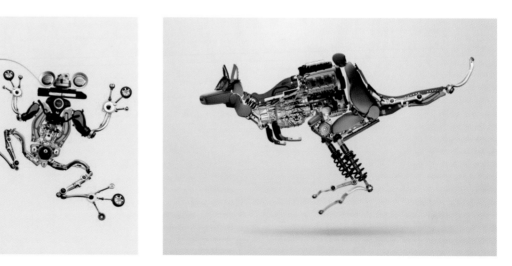

Client: Audi Agency: Bartle Bogle Hegarty (BBH),London AD: Matt Kemsley Photo: Kevin Summers

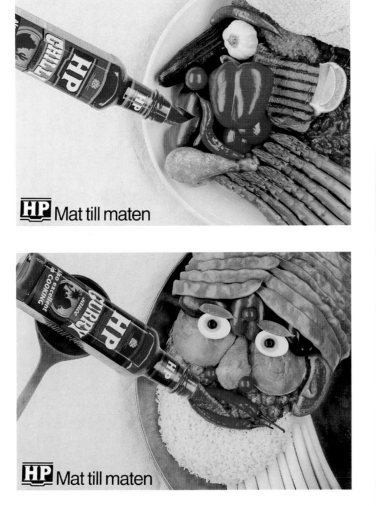

HP **Mat till maten**

HP **Mat till maten**

'HP: Food for your dinner.'

Client: HP Agency: Saatchi & Saatchi, Copenhagen AD: Eric Ericson, Anders Krisár Photo: Tessa Traeger

HP **Mat till maten**

HP **Mat till maten**

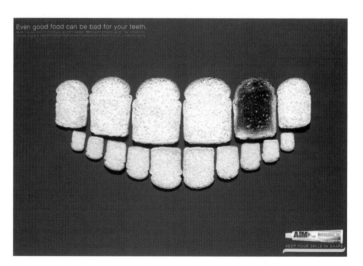

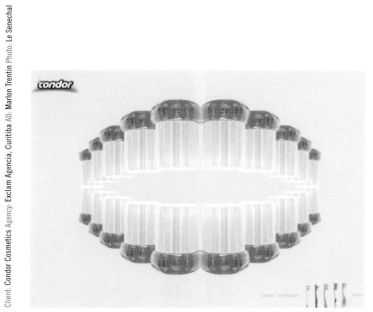

Poster announcing a
Girl Scouts of America
'Luau' event, based on
a traditional Hawaiian
festival. The cookie is
broken into the shape of
the Hawaiian islands.

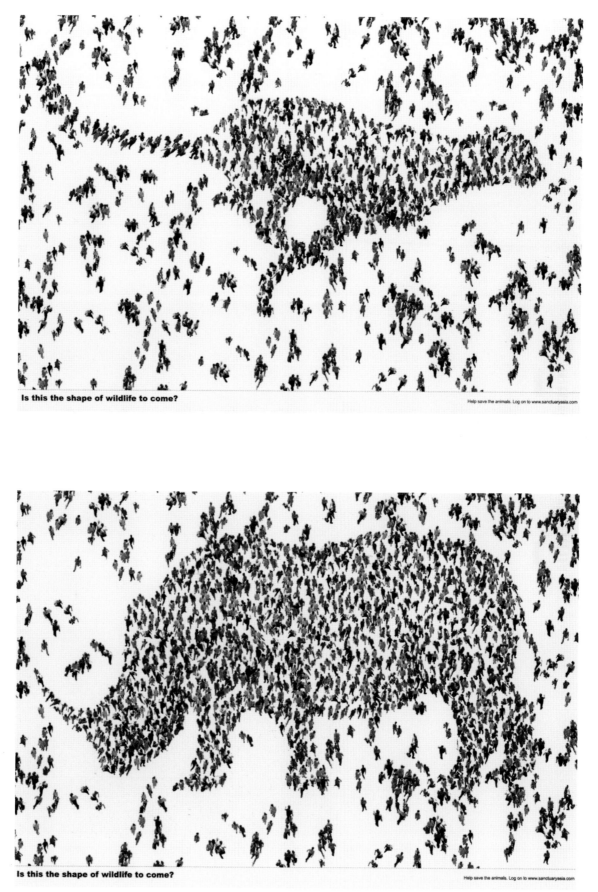

Is this the shape of wildlife to come?

Help save the animals. Log on to www.sanctuaryasia.com

Is this the shape of wildlife to come?

Help save the animals. Log on to www.sanctuaryasia.com

Client: Sanctuary Asia Magazine Agency: Ambience Publicis, Mumbai AD: Uday Parkar Photo: Atul Patil

Ad for the German railway system.

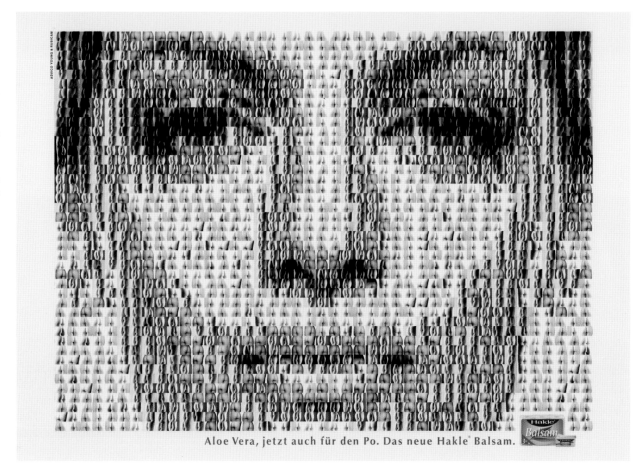

Client: Hakle Agency: Advico Young & Rubicam, Zurich AD: Roland Scotoni

Aloe Vera, jetzt auch für den Po. Das neue Hakle® Balsam.

'Aloe Vera, now also for the bottom. The new Hakle Balsam.'

An estate agent's ad with a mosaic of buildings.

Client: vasakronan.se Agency: Jersild, Wessman & Enander, Stockholm AD: Marita Kuntonen Photo: Hans Gedda

Official sponsors of
the European Football
Championships 2004.
The picture is made up
of the flags of all the
participating nations.

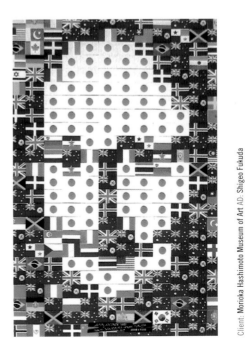

A Japanese art gallery.

Setting up a scene
means playing with the
established modes of
seeing. The examples
on the following pages
show how easy it is
to manipulate human
perception. Because
we are conditioned
by particular shapes,
common images, certain
key stimuli, familiar

#6 SETTING UP A SCENE

colour combinations
and patterns, these
scenes force us to make
formal associations
with things that are not
actually illustrated, or
only indirectly so. 'How'
something is shown
becomes more important
than 'what' is shown.

quattro®

Vorsprung durch Technik www.audi.at

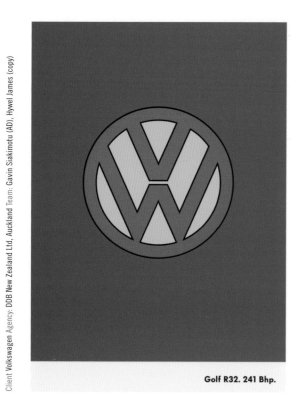

Golf R32. 241 Bhp.

VW dressed as Superman.

Lunch time.

Der BMW X5 4.4i

Print wirkt.

Print wirkt.

The 'Print Works' series uses designs from striking and well-known ad campaigns in order to show the effectiveness of print.

TIME TO RUN:
26.9.2004
31. BERLIN-MARATHON

TIME TO RUN:
26.9.2004
31. BERLIN-MARATHON

Ads for a sports shoe specialist.

This laptop with
its prominent handle
is camouflaged
among the handbags.
'A bagful of fun'.

Erdal shoe polish.

Client: TA-Media Agency: McCann-Erickson, Zurich AD: Nicolas Vontobel, Tom Kees

A weekly newspaper with small ads for cars. 'The safest way to your dream car is through the new Fahrzeugtipp, the biggest weekly motor market in Switzerland. Every Saturday in the *Tages-Anzeiger.*'

Der sicherste Weg zu Ihrem Wunschauto führt über den neuen Fahrzeugtipp, den grössten wöchentlichen Fahrzeugmarkt der Schweiz. Jeden Samstag im Tages-Anzeiger. **Tages Anzeiger**

Der schnellste Weg zu Ihrem Wunschauto führt über den neuen Fahrzeugtipp, den grössten wöchentlichen Fahrzeugmarkt der Schweiz. Jeden Samstag im Tages-Anzeiger. **Tages Anzeiger**

Client: Teflon Agency: Young & Rubicam, São Paulo AD: Denis Kakazu Photo: João Avila

Teflon®. Protects your clothes against water, oil and dirt.

Teflon®. Protects your clothes against water, oil and dirt.

Client: Vizir Agency: Leo Burnett, Warsaw AD: Martin Winther Photo: Darek Zatorski

JAPANESE DESIGNER-FASHION. EMIS, WILDPRETMARKT 7, 1010 WIEN

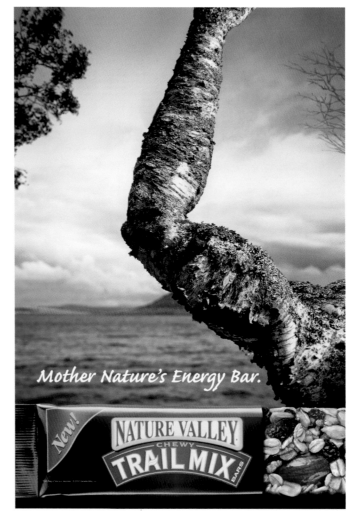

Mother Nature's Energy Bar.

Client: Nature Valley Agency: Cossette Communication-Marketing, Montreal AD: Gerald Schoenhoff Photo: Darran Rees

Client: Neutrogena Agency: DDB, Hong Kong AD: Thomas Chung Photo: Thomas Chung

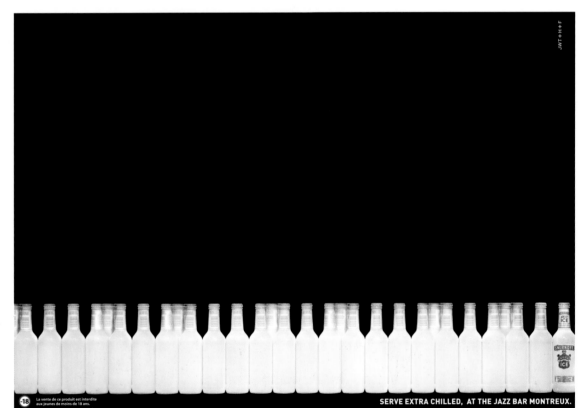

Client: Süddeutsche Zeitung GmbH Agency: GBK, Heye Werbeagentur, Munich AD: Felix Hennermann Photo: Jan Willem Scholten

A piano shop. 'Hear the world with different eyes.'

Client: DIAGEO Swiss SA Agency: JWT + Hostettler + Fabrikant, Zurich AD: Nici Vontobel Photo: df

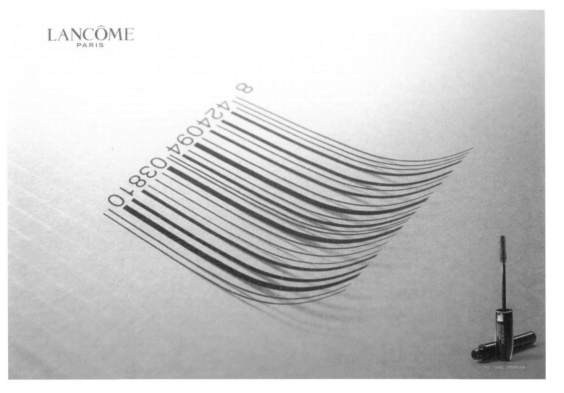

LANCÔME
PARIS

Client: Lancôme Paris Agency: Publicis, Madrid AD: Luis Solero Photo: José Luis Mora

Eye shadow.
'The third dimension'.

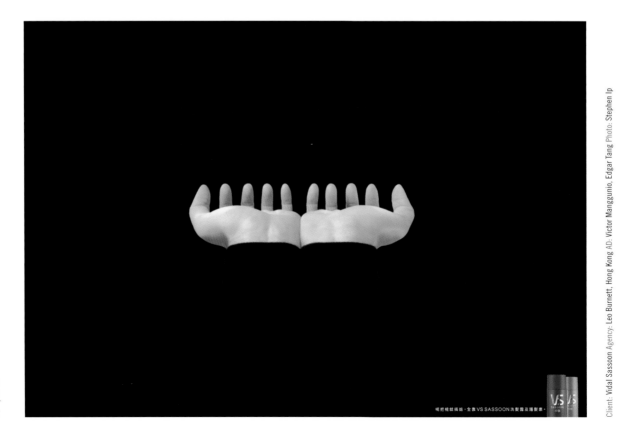

'No matter what
mess your hair is
in, this "comb"
will deal with it.'

Client: Vidal Sassoon Agency: Leo Burnett, Hong Kong AD: Victor Mangunio, Edgar Tang Photo: Stephen Ip

Only the finest of fish. (DINE)

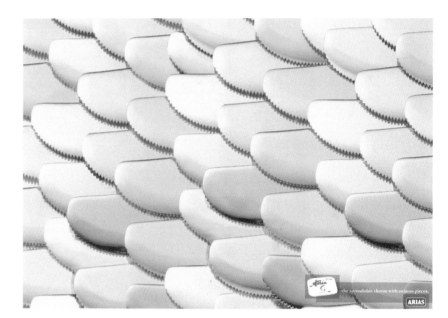

60971729 4165717240097

BATESITALIA THE SELLING IDEA

An Italian ad agency,
advertising itself.

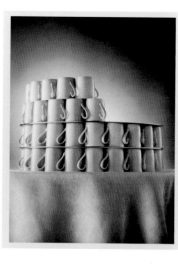

Italian coffee. The cups
are arranged to form the
Colosseum in Rome and
the Leaning Tower of Pisa.

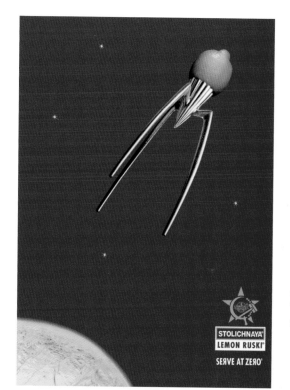

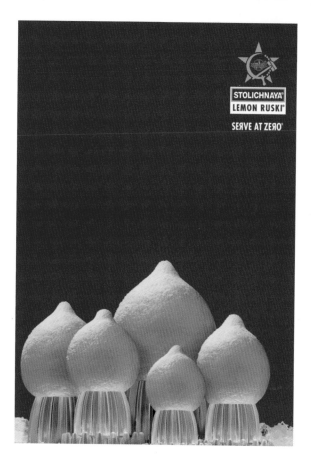

In translation, this
packet soup is called
'Knorr Long Tongue'.

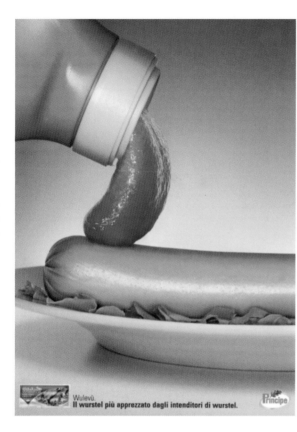

Wulevù.
Il wurstel più apprezzato dagli intenditori di wurstel.

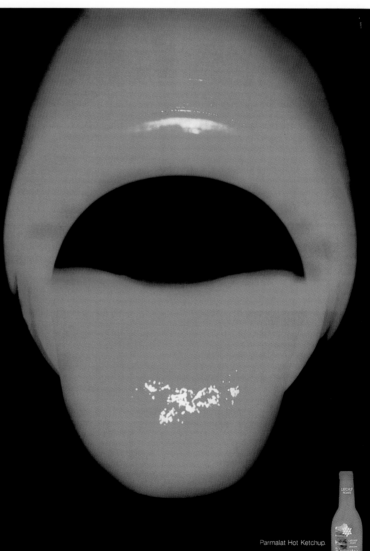

Parmalat Hot Ketchup.

FLIMS
LAAX
FALERA©

DIE ALPENARENA

250 km Wanderwege.
Und 70 Restaurants zum Auftanken. www.alpenarena.ch

Ad for a Swiss
holiday resort.
'250 km of footpaths.
And 70 restaurants
for refuelling.'

DIE BRILLE MACHT DAS GESICHT.

KRASS
OPTIK

DIE BRILLE MACHT DAS GESICHT.

KRASS
OPTIK

'The glasses make the face.'

Vin de Pologne

FAMOUS POTATO VODKA

Ad for a toilet cleaner
with added air freshener.

Two different butters
with sea salt.

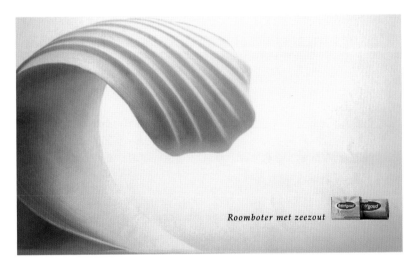

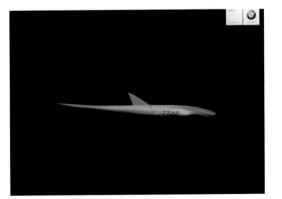

'Ecological washing'.

ÖKOLOGISCHER WASCHEN

Client: Cesar Agency: Attack CMG, Singapore AD: Priscilla Sim Photo: Lee Jen

New Cesar Chicken Supreme. Now with a delicious topping of vegetables.

Two flavours of dog food
with added vegetables.

New Cesar Gourmet Beef. Now with a delicious topping of vegetables.

'There's no substitute for meat.' Ads for a restaurant.

Client: Esplanada Grill Agency: Lew Lara Propaganda, São Paulo AD: Carlos Nunes Photo: Luis Moretti

'Anything that can fall needs protection. Wear a cycle helmet.' Ad for an insurance company.

Client: Suva Schweizerische Unfallversicherung Agency: Ruf Lanz Werbeagentur AG, Zurich Concept: Markus Ruf, Danielle Lanz Photo: Stefan Minder, Felix Schregenberger

Client: Reebok Agency: Saatchi & Saatchi, Singapore AD: Simon Cox Photo: Ian Butterworth

Running shoes with
reflectors for night-time
(above) and extremely
lightweight
cross-trainers (below).

www.playboy.nl

Manix° condoms. Partner of female pleasure.

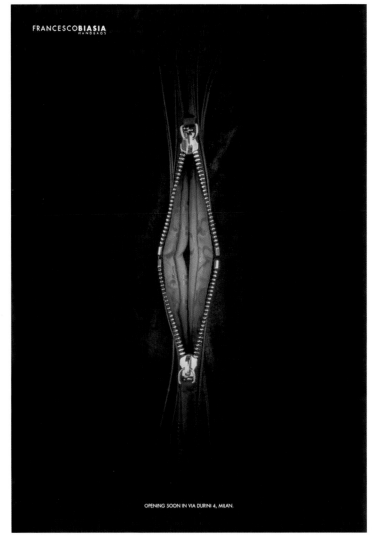

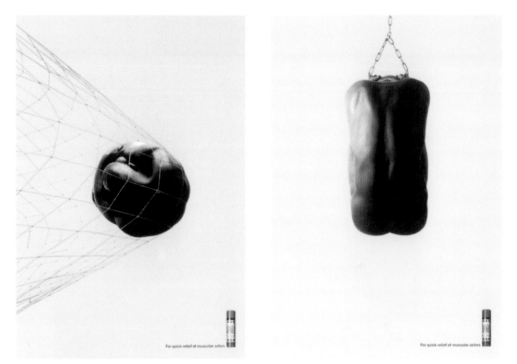

Client: Deep Health Agency: Saatchi & Saatchi, Singapore AD: Larry Ong Photo: Vincent Koh

'The power of Lynx.'

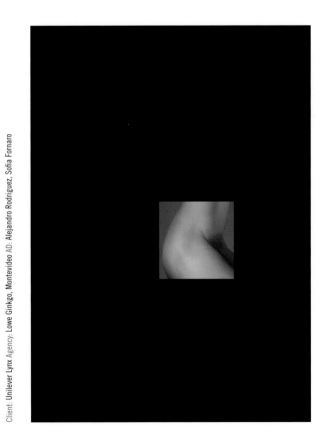

Client: Unilever Lynx Agency: Lowe Ginkgo, Montevideo AD: Alejandro Rodriguez, Sofia Fornaro

'My slimming partner'.

Client: **Contrex** Agency: **Australia, Paris** AD: **Thierry Fevre** Photo: **Viktor Polson**

Your feet can be sexy too.

Summer Collection 2002
VIA UNO

Client: **Via Uno** Agency: **Tropa Grey, Santiago de Chile** AD: **Damian Balmaceda** Photo: **René Zúniga**

Client: The Economist Agency: Ogilvy & Mather, Singapore AD: Richard Johnson, Kelly Dickinson, Naoki Ga, Craig Smith Photo: Roy Zhang

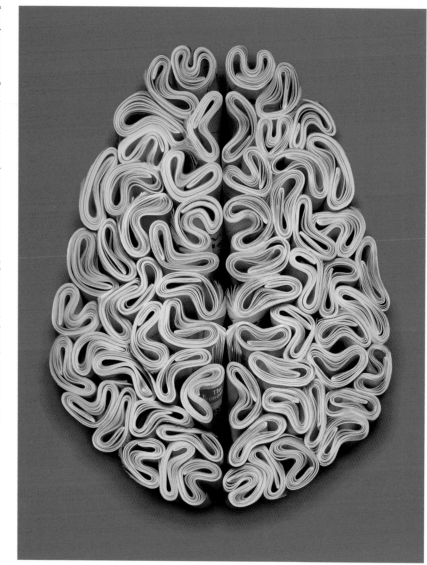

'Stop thinking about it, and
buy yourself a mobile.'

Client: Diax Agency: McCann Erickson, Zurich AD: Nicolas Vontobel, Martin Bettler

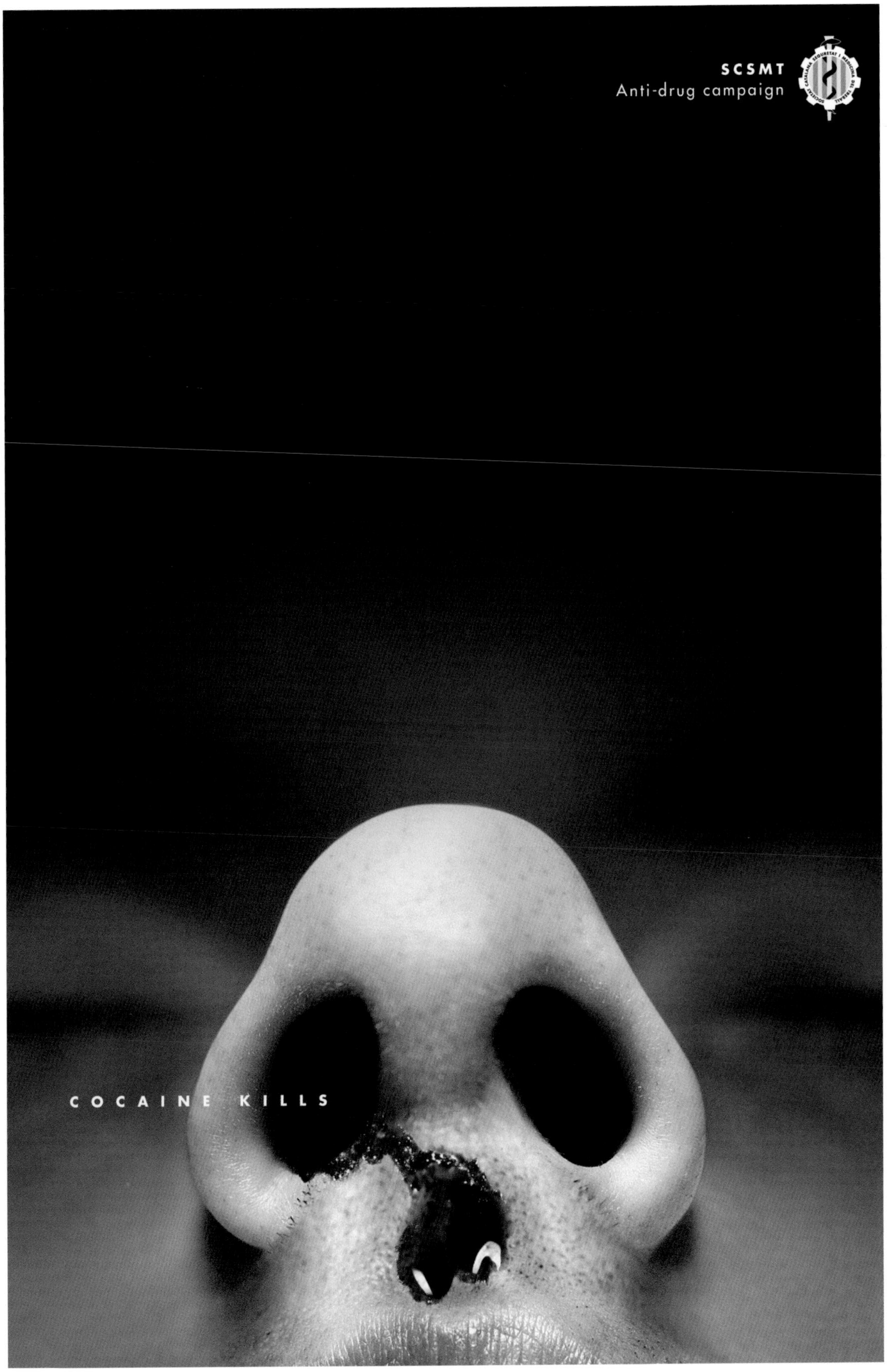

SCSMT
Anti-drug campaign

COCAINE KILLS

Client: SCSMT Agency: Bassat Ogilvy, Madrid AD: Francesc Talamino Photo: Joan Garrigosa

The images in this
chapter lead a double
life. At first glance, they
are seen for what they
actually are. However,
the interpretation of
what is 'seen' changes at
the moment when some
additional information
is received. This may, for
example, stem from the
theme of the campaign,
or from the copy. Because
of this extra information,
the whole context takes
on a totally new meaning,

#7 SEEING IN CONTEXT

and what has been
seen appears in a very
different light. The new
interpretation is stored,
and from that moment
on it is impossible to
repeat the spontaneous
view that one had at the
beginning. With some of
the examples, however,
there will be some
observers who see straight
away what others will only
perceive by means of the
additional context.

Client: Heineken Agency: Leo Burnett, Bangkok AD: Prayuth Jaturonrusmi Photo: Fahdol Na Nagara

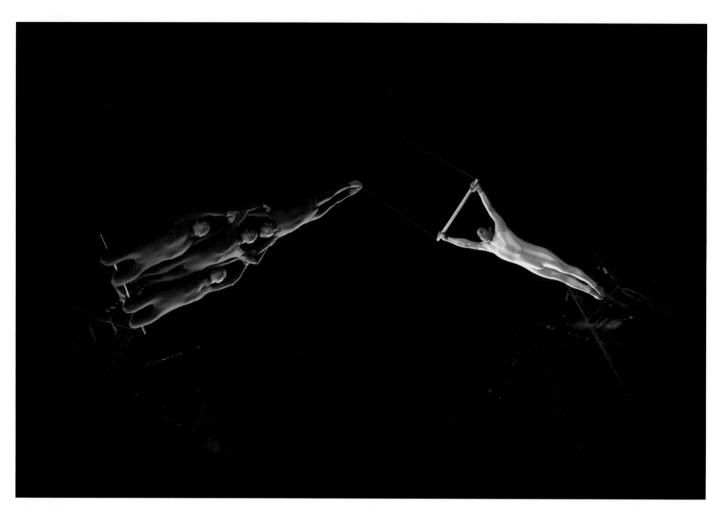

Heineken beer with
its characteristic green
bottle and a bottle-opener.
Heineken were sponsoring
a circus festival.

Burlington socks with
their checked pattern
and trademark button.

Client: Burlington Agency: Springer & Jacoby Werbung, Hamburg AD: Birgit Hogrefe Photo: Birgit Hogrefe

ABSOLUT AMSTERDAM.

ABSOLUT VLADIVOSTOK.

ABSOLUT ROME.

ABSOLUT PURITY.

ABSOLUT OBSESSION.

ABSOLUT SPACE.

Over twenty years of
ads, the Absolut vodka
bottle has been given
many new forms.

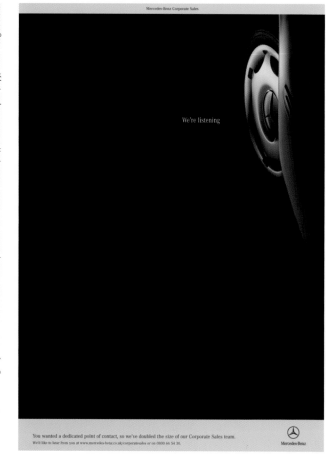

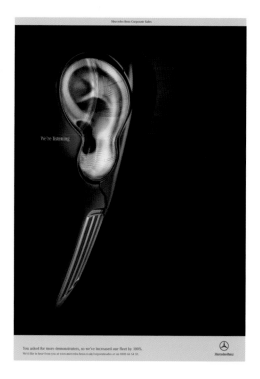

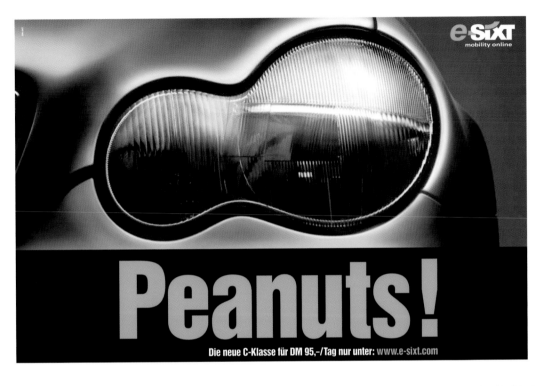

e·SiXT
mobility online

Peanuts!

Die neue C-Klasse für DM 95,–/Tag nur unter: www.e-sixt.com

In 1994, a spokesman for the board of the Deutsche Bank, after a spectacular bankruptcy case involving a construction form, described the sum of 50 million marks as 'peanuts'. This was regarded as the gaffe of the year, but entered everyday language in Germany. Here the car-hire firm Sixt has taken it up again, linking it to the shape of the headlight and, of course, the price of their rentals.

New beetle Ⓥ

Ⓥ

Don't worry.

Der New Beetle Ⓥ

The online clinic for mothers to be. **WebBaby**.co.uk

Campaign by the
Norwegian Ministry
of Transport.

Client: Statens Vegvesen Agency: Dinamo, Lysaker, Oslo Team: Henrik Habberstad (CD), Jennie-Ann Johansson (AD) Photo: Massimo Leardini

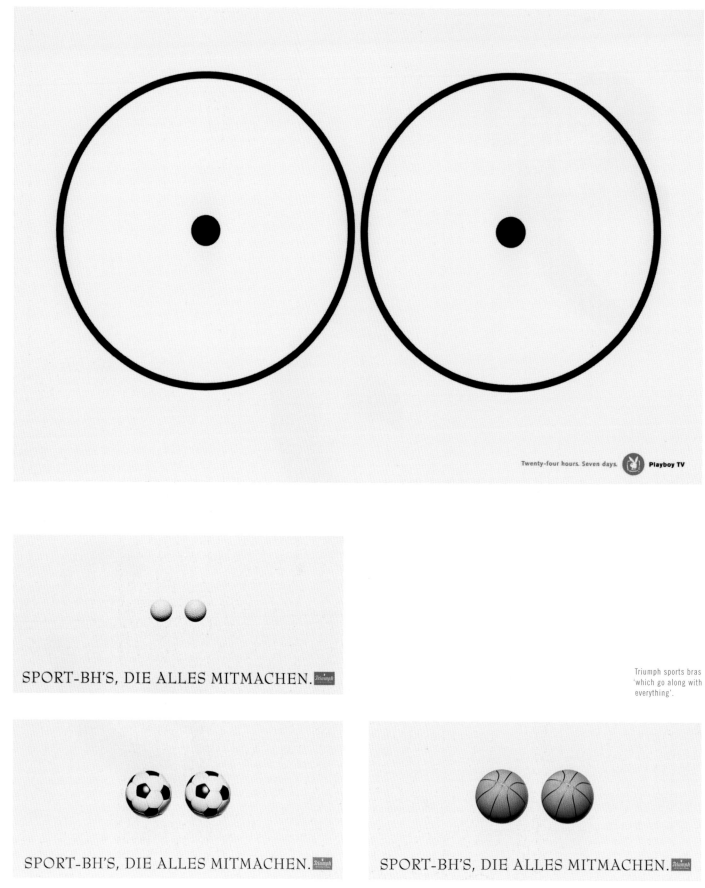

Twenty-four hours. Seven days. Playboy TV

SPORT-BH'S, DIE ALLES MITMACHEN. Triumph

Triumph sports bras 'which go along with everything'.

SPORT-BH'S, DIE ALLES MITMACHEN. Triumph

SPORT-BH'S, DIE ALLES MITMACHEN. Triumph

THE ONE AND ONLY
wonderbra

we do know now what Eiffel had in mind when he designed the tower.

lingerie made in Paris

Ad for French
lingerie. 'We do know
now what Eiffel
had in mind when he
designed the tower.'

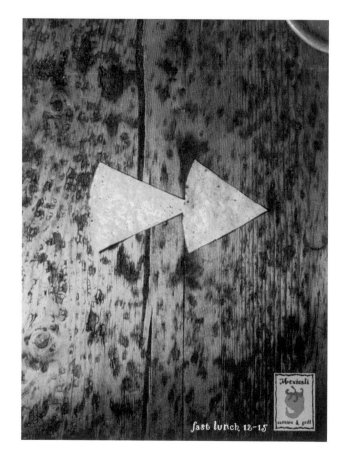

Client: Mexicali Agency: Racing Pigeons, Milan AD: Giovanni Settesoldi Photo: Riccardo Bagnoli

Mexican restaurant.

Client: Sushi kin Agency: DM9 DDB, São Paulo AD: Roberto Fernandez Photo: Rafael Costa

Japanese restaurant.

Client: Guinness Agency: Abbott Mead Vickers BBDO, London
AD: Paul Brazier, Huw Williams Photo: Tim O'Sullivan

Guinness are always
finding new ways
of depicting the
dark brew with the
white head.

Das Beste aus Trauben.

Weinhandel R. K. Schmidt
Französische Weine aus Eigenimporten www.weine-von-aschhorn.de

Das Beste aus Trauben.

Weinhandel R. K. Schmidt
Französische Weine aus Eigenimporten www.weine-von-aschhorn.de

'The best of grapes.'

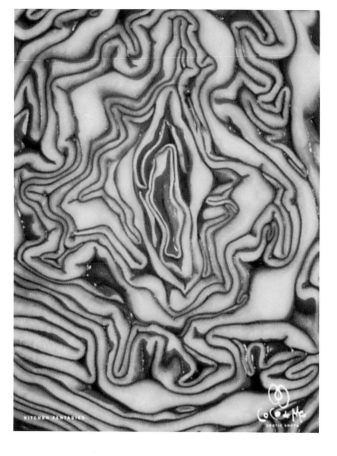

Coco de Mer
erotic shops.

'Pupille glasses and
contact lenses.'

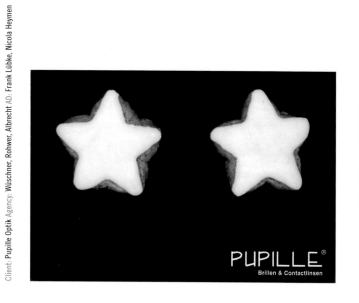

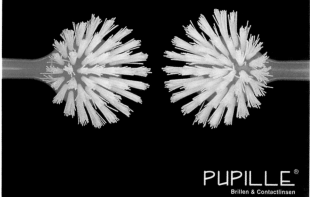

'Chips at the Cathedral.'

Energy bars with fruit.

'Ikea. More parking
spaces. New store
opening in Graz.'

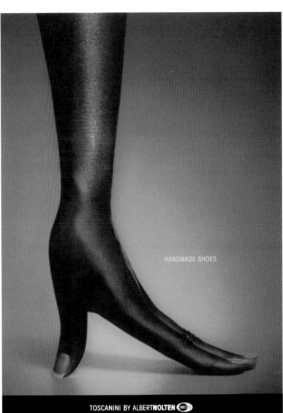

HANDMADE SHOES

TOSCANINI BY ALBERT**NOLTEN**

DEN HAAG   DELFT   LEIDSCHENDAM   WWW.NOLTEN.NL

Schuhe, die anziehen.

Blicker.

These German ads
for shoes are a play
on words: 'anziehen'
means to put on, and
also to attract.

Schuhe, die anziehen.

Blicker.

Schuhe, die anziehen.

Blicker.

Client: Blasón Decaf Agency: Nazca Saatchi & Saatchi, Mexico City AD: Pascual García

Good night!

Blasón

Decaf

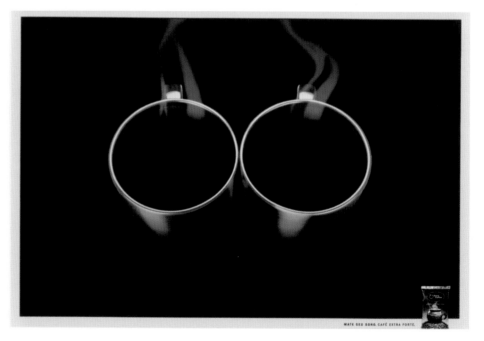

Extra strong coffee.

Client: Black Coffee Agency: Rio Propaganda, Niteroi AD: Ronnie Vlcek Photo: Guido Paternó

Raspberry flavored coffee

CAFE DEL
MONDO

Best Brasilian blend

CAFE DEL
MONDO

WE'RE ON DUTY, EVEN AT LUNCHTIME.
YOUR SWISS PEUGEOT DEALER.

The Toyota Spacio is
a seven-seater van.

Washing-up liquid.
'Amazingly bright dishes'.

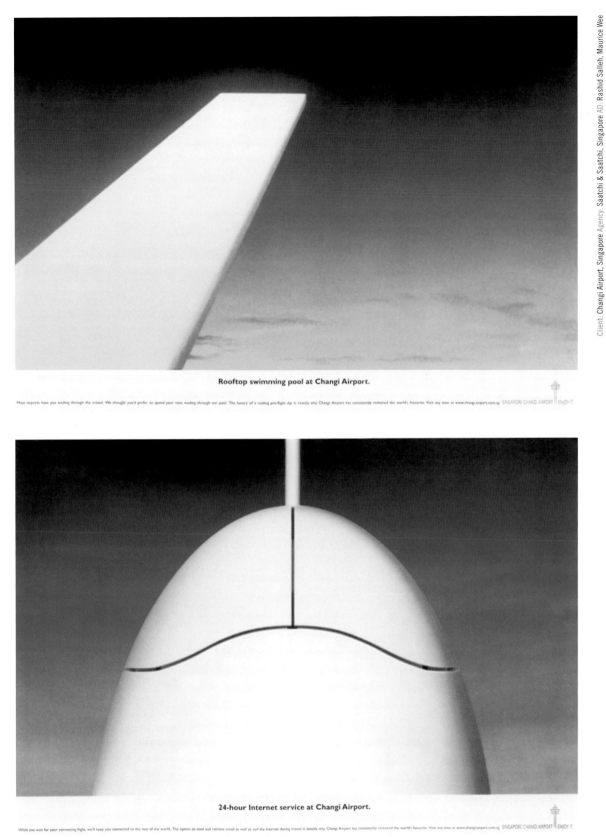

Rooftop swimming pool at Changi Airport.

Most airports have you wading through the crowd. We thought you'd prefer to spend your time wading through our pool. The luxury of a cooling pre-flight dip is exactly why Changi Airport has consistently remained the world's favourite. Visit any time at www.changi.airport.com.sg SINGAPORE CHANGI AIRPORT ENJOY IT

24-hour Internet service at Changi Airport.

While you wait for your connecting flight, we'll keep you connected to the rest of the world. The option to send and retrieve email as well as surf the Internet during transit is exactly why Changi Airport has consistently remained the world's favourite. Visit any time at www.changi.airport.com.sg SINGAPORE CHANGI AIRPORT ENJOY IT

Client: Changi Airport, Singapore Agency Saatchi & Saatchi, Singapore AD: Rashid Salleh, Maurice Wee

When we look around, our eyes tend to focus on outlines and anything that breaks into them or overlaps them. The outline is the border between the figure and the ground, or between the object and the space around it. The immense importance of outlines can be seen from the fact that a simple line is enough for us to identify an object easily and with complete certainty.

#8 OUTLINES

Many brands and products have succeeded in planting their image so firmly in our memories that they can be identified by means of their shape alone. In the second part of this chapter, you will see some 'subjective' outlines. Our knowledge of these is taken so much for granted that our brains can fill them in, even when they don't exist.

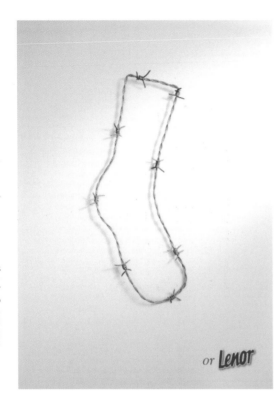

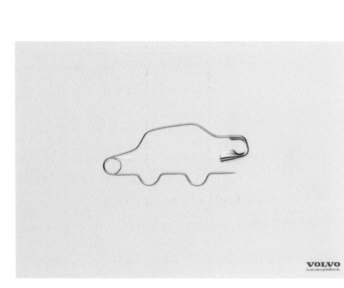

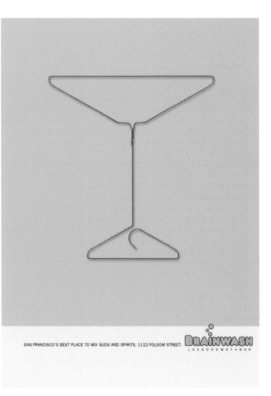

Think of a soft drink.

Think of a french perfume.

Think of a chocolate snack bar

Think of a potato chips brand

TDH: THE POWER OF DESIGN.

Client: TDH Design Company Agency: Cathedral the Creative Center, Madrid

 Client: Peugeot Agency: BETC Euro RSCG, Paris AD: Joann Ameline

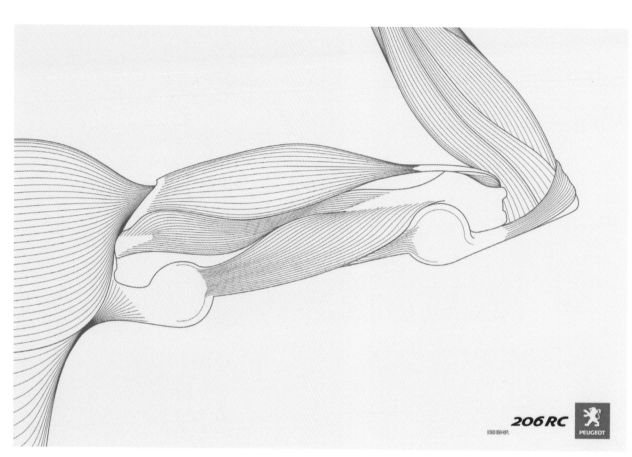

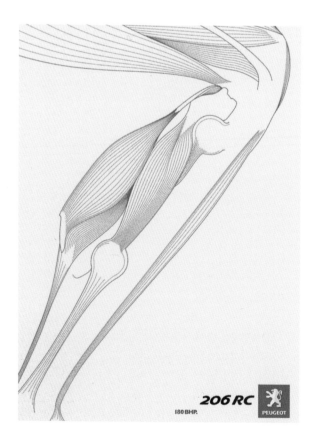

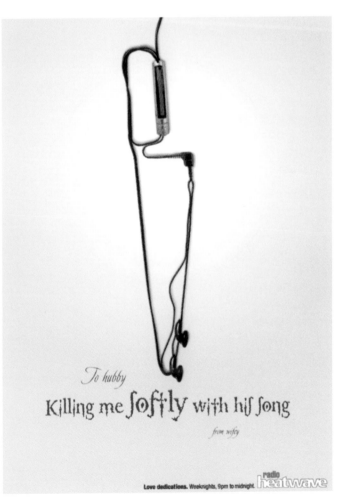

Client: **Radio Heatwave** Agency: **Eryk Tam, Singapore** AD: **Eryk Tam** Photo: **Eryk Tam**

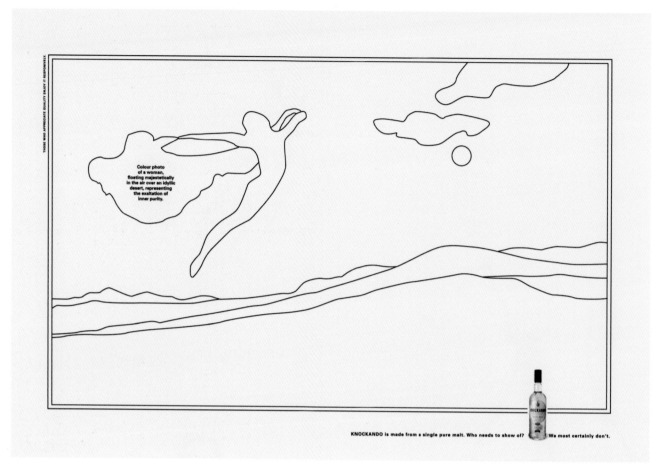

Colour photo
of a woman,
floating majestetically
in the air over an idyllic
desert, representing
the exaltation of
inner purity.

KNOCKANDO is made from a single pure malt. Who needs to show of? We most certainly don't.

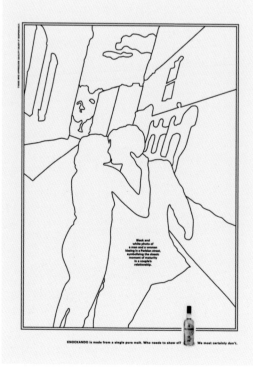

'Black and white
photo of a man and
a woman kissing in
a Parisian street,
symbolizing the
classic moment of
maturity in a couple's
relationship.'

Client: UBS Realty Agency: ADK Kyushu, Fukuoka City AD: Koichiro Nishihata Photo: Akira Kitajima

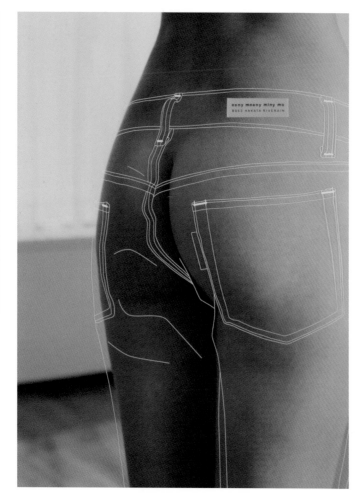 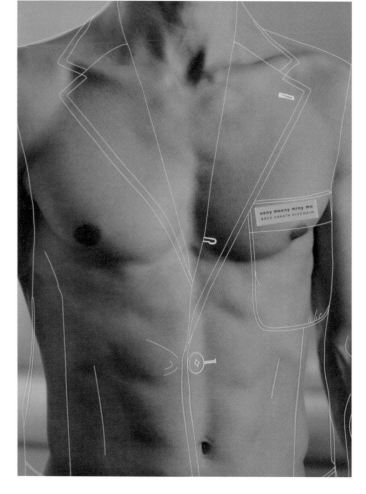

Property investment
consultancy.

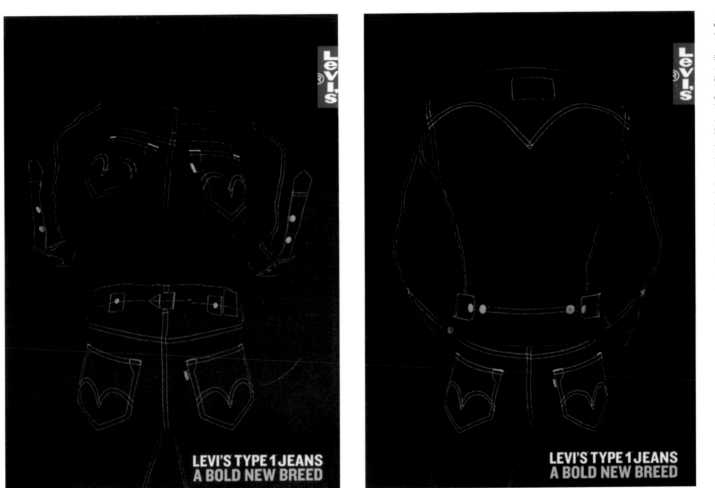

Client: Levi's Agency: Bartle Bogle Hegarty, London AD: Joseph Ernst Photo: Warren du Preez

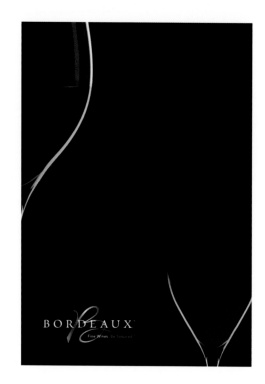

'Bordeaux.
Fine wines.
Be seduced.'

By giving web addresses
and not naming the
brand, this campaign
directs people to the
relevant product
website of Wehkamp,
Holland's biggest
online warehouse.

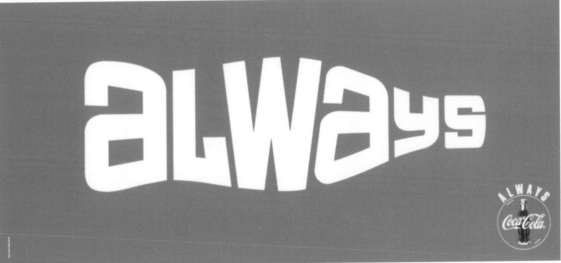

Client: Coca-Cola Agency: McCann-Erickson, Zurich AD: Edi Andrist

Client: Cotton Council International Agency: DDB Needham, Hong Kong AD: Wally Leung, Danny Wong, Edmond Chan Photo: Mihael Lee

'Really natural.'

真自然 真感覺

真自然 真感覺

真自然 真感覺

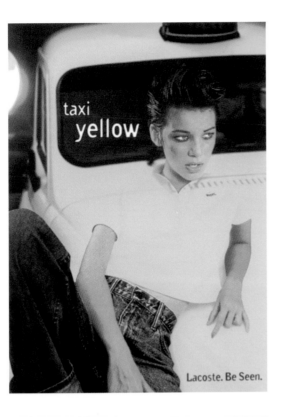

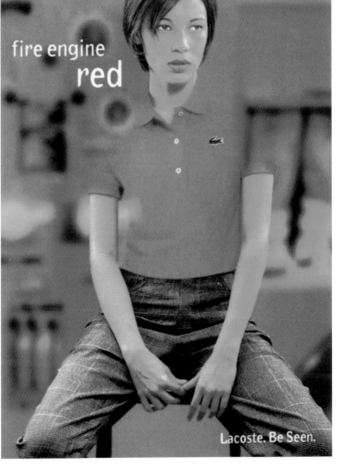

Client: Lacoste Agency: Wunderman Cato Johnson, Singapore AD: Koh Kuan Eng Photo: Chuan Do

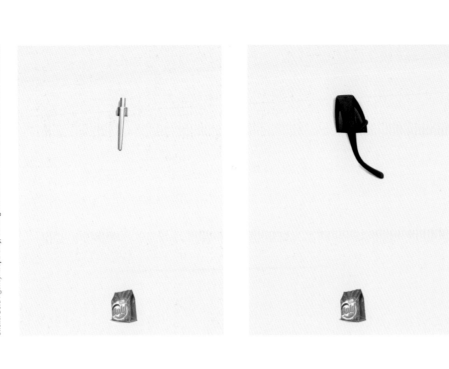

Ads for a shoe store.

GUINNESS

Think positive!

It has a tendency to disappear.

Client: BMW Agency: Jung von Matt, Hamburg AD: Tobias Eichinger Photo: Uwe Düttmann

'We know your BMW.'

In this commercial for
a cleaning fluid, we
see men pretending to
carry a sheet of glass
through the town,
and the reactions of
the passers-by.

Client: Lever Fabergé Deutschland Agency: Springer & Jacoby, Hamburg AD: Rolf Leger

1: Hush Puppies, USA 2: Seatrain Lines-Shipping Company, USA 3: Kamijima Cardiology Clinic, Japan 4: NBA, USA 5: Nova Medics, Japan 6: Cinetex-Motion pictures, USA 7: Eaton Corporation - Small Engine Part and Truck manufacturer, USA

The technique of creating objects by leaving things out is a favourite among graphic artists and painters, but it requires precise knowledge of how our brains construct the things we perceive.

The fact that words
and pictures are closely
connected was clear
long before the arrival
of emoticons. After all,
writing itself originated
through systems of
symbols. Perhaps that's
why it's so much fun to
mix the two together
or replace one with
the other. Deciphering
hybrid combinations is

#9 WORDS AND PICTURES

no problem. The design
potential of words and
pictures is wide-ranging
and extremely attractive.
This can be seen from
the many variations
illustrated in this
chapter. On the following
pages you will find a
collection of the most
fascinating word games
that designers play.

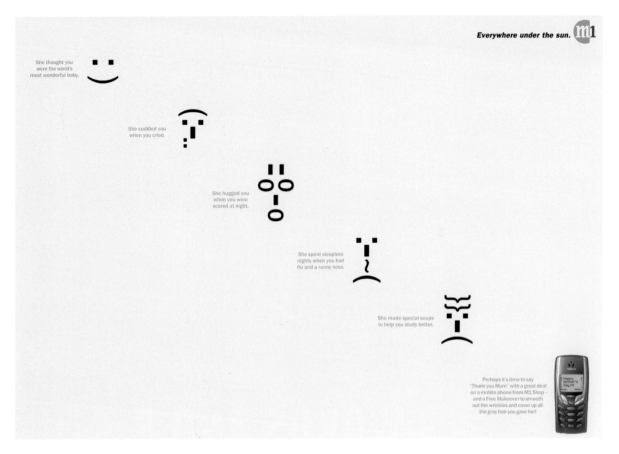

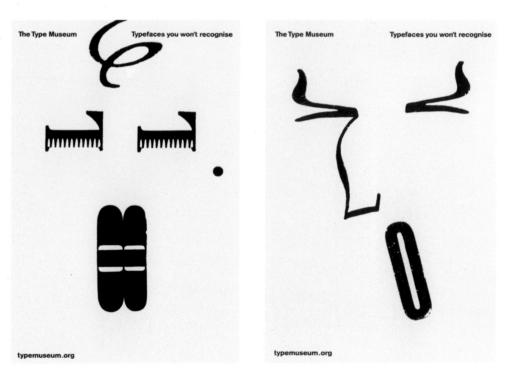

Client: Veja Magazine Agency: Almap BBDO, São Paulo Team: Roberto Fernandez (AD), Sophie Schoenburg

Client: GEO Agency: Kolle Rebbe, Hamburg AD: Julia Otten

Poster for special edition of *GeoEpoche*: '11 September 2001: the day the world changed'

The shadow thrown
by the chillis spells
out the name of the
cigarette brand.

French beer: 1664 Kronenbourg. 'Four
figures – stronger than all words.'

Sunday edition of the
Neue Züricher Zeitung.
'To enjoy with reason.'

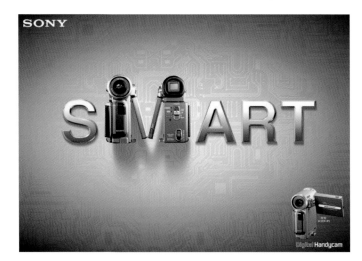

National Theatre, Lisbon.
'Pure emotion'.

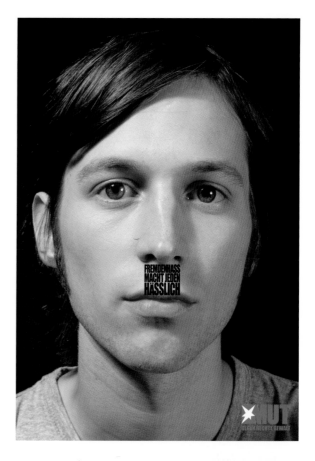

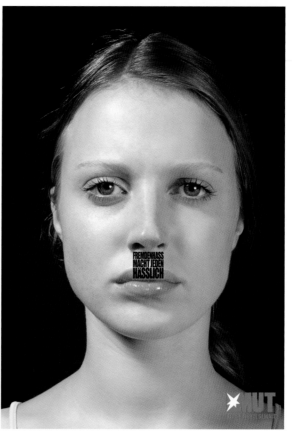

Stern magazine's
campaign against
right-wing violence:
'Xenophobia makes
everyone ugly.'

Die Bahn **DB**

(Piep) „Auf den Autobahnen A1 bis A995 bildet sich auch heute ein Stau von insgesamt 1.000 km. Wir empfehlen allen Autofahrern, die Störung weiträumig zu umfahren." (Piep) **Steigen Sie ein. Am Bahnhof in Ihrer Nähe, über die Reisebüros mit DB-Lizenz oder unter www.bahn.de**

Ad for the German
railway system.
The text of a traffic
report takes the
shape and colour
of a German train.

Ad for a café
and bookstore.

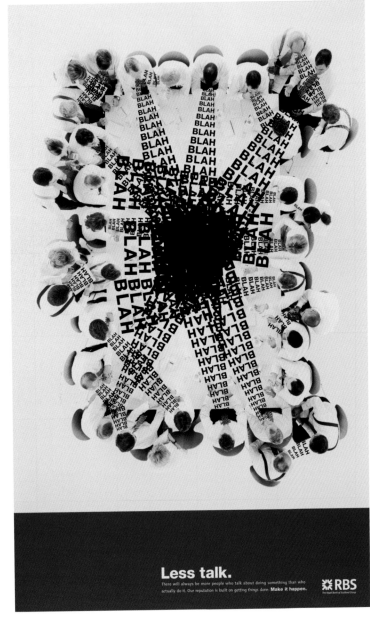

Advice from an international
financial services company.

Client: Volvo Agency: TBWA/EPG, Lisbon AD: António Belchio

Client: Patrick O'Hara Salon Agency: Slingshot, Dallas AD: Sok-kien Chen

Decaffeinated
instant coffee.

Client: Nescafé Agency: McCann-Erickson, Madrid AD: Inaki Bendito

Ad for a ski resort.
The trail of words
highlights its
various features.

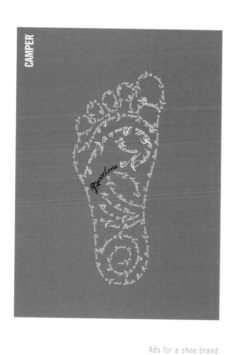

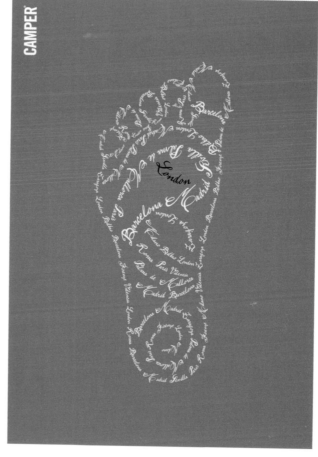

Ads for a shoe brand.

'Whatever happens, you're right there with us.' The slogan of the German newspaper *Bild* is a play on words. 'Bild' means picture, but the complete slogan means 'Form your own opinion'.

Client: Axel Springer AG Agency: Jung von Matt, Hamburg AD: Hans Weishäupl

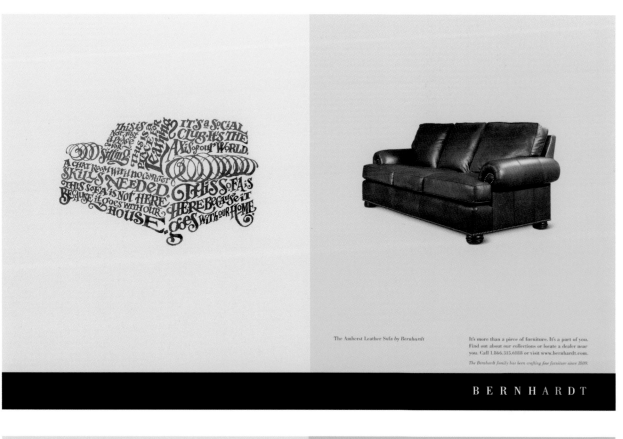

Valor is a business newspaper:
'Don't get lost in the world of numbers.'

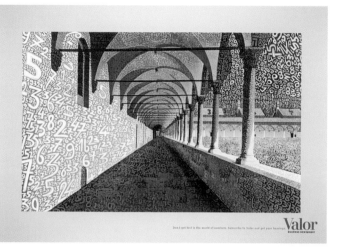

Ad for the German magazine *Stern*: 'We give
news a face. Keep things in perspective.'

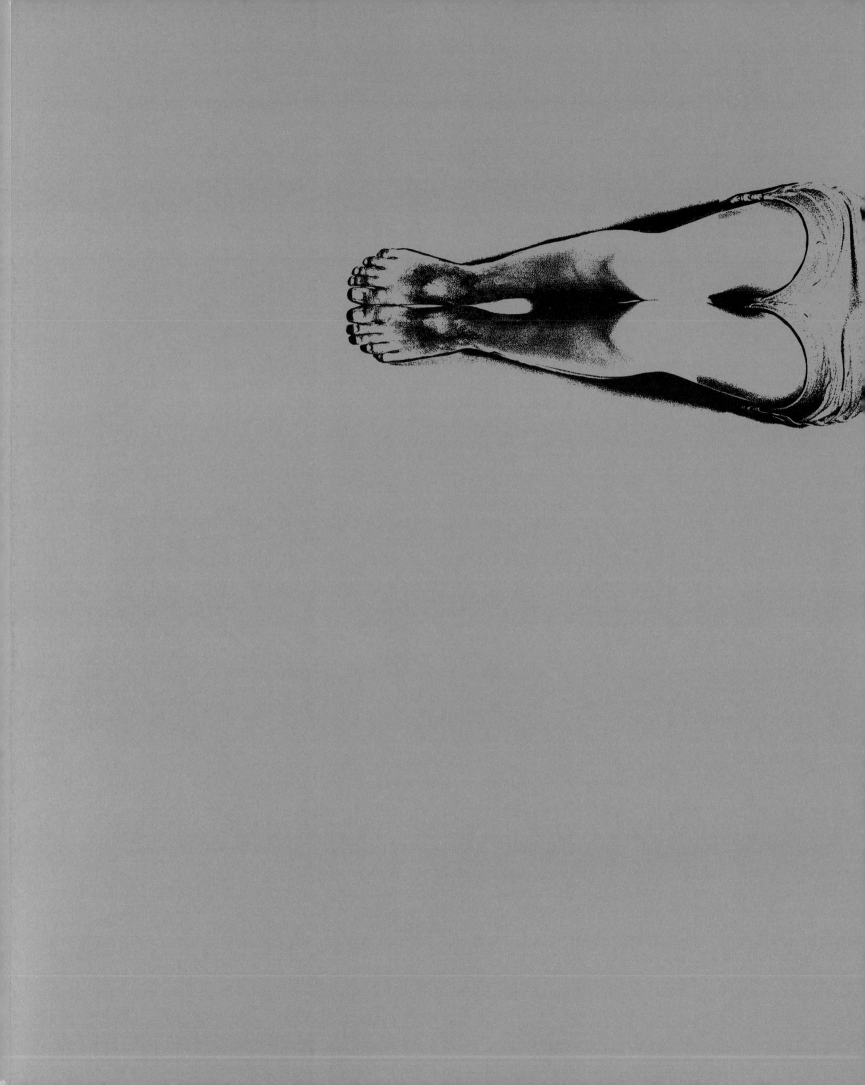

This chapter is a homage to the genius loci, the spirit of the place, and the boundless desire to construct that characterizes the sense of sight. Here the frontier between the medium and its environment is totally transcended. Normally ignored by both the designer and the observer, now the surroundings become

#10 ON THE SPOT

part of the idea. Existing elements are seized upon and set in such a way that the observer's mind creates a collage of meanings. For instance, the doors of a bus turn into a shark's jaws, an exhaust pipe becomes a cigarette, and the staples in the centre of a magazine, which you usually never notice, catch not only the tights but also the reader's eye.

Pulligan Pantyhose Strong Series **PULLIGAN**

FOREVER SPORT

adidas

'Beautiful hats.'

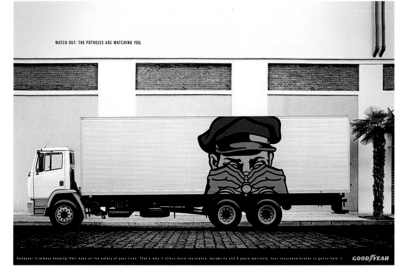

Client: **Bharat Petroleum** Agency: **Saatchi & Saatchi, Mumbai** AD: **Kalpesh Patankar**

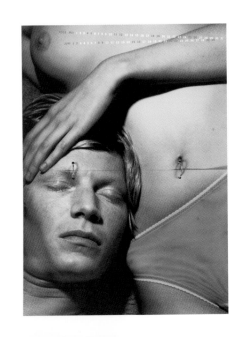

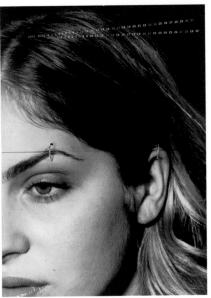

Client: meridianspa Agency: Weigertpirouzwolf, Hamburg AD: Kaja Franke

Client: Endless Pain Tattoo & Piercing Studio Agency: Weigertpirouzwolf, Hamburg AD: Barbara Schirmer Photo: Hans Starck

Calendar for a tattoo
and piercing studio.

Advert for a piercing
studio in Oslo.

Client: Oslo Piercing Studio Agency: Leo Burnett, Oslo AD: Erik Heisholt, Marianne Heckmann

Client: Amnesty International Agency: TBWA, Paris AD: Philippe Taroux

Client: Sportplausch Wider Agency: Publicis, Zurich AD: Ralph Halder

Ad for a sports shop:
'High time for some
keep-fit kit.'

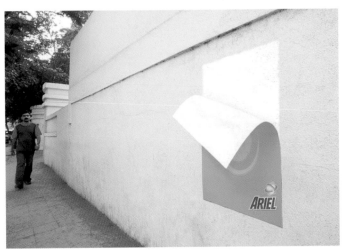

Client: Ariel Agency: Saatchi & Saatchi, Mumbai AD: Shantanu Pisolkar

Client: **NSPCC (National Society for the Prevention of Cruelty to Children)** Agency: Saatchi & Saatchi, London AD: Dave Hilyard

Client: **La Mote** Agency: Bold/TBWA, Oslo AD: Stephanie Dumont

Ad for low-cost holidays:
'Better to be drinking sangria!'

Ad for protein supplement.

Können Sie auch so denken?

A business consultancy advertising for applicants: 'Can you think like this too?'

Client: National Geographic Channel Agency: Amsterdam Advertising AD: Darre van Dijk

Ad for a documentary
about sharks.

Client: Smint Agency: Tandem Campmany Guasch DDB, Barcelona

Ad for mints:
'No Smint, no kiss.'

Client: HTM Agency: D'Arcy, Amsterdam AD: Darre van Dijk

One of the largest local public
transport companies in the
Netherlands: 'The stress-free way
to the North Sea Jazz festival?
Take the bus or the tram.'

'Load a lot,
consume
just a few.'

Client: Volkswagen Agency: DDB Argentina, Buenos Aires

Before the trees
blossom, this ad
shows the colours that
will soon be visible.
The accuracy of the
forecast is shown
by the blossoms.

Client: Flughafen Nürnberg Service GmbH Agency: Springer & Jacoby, Hamburg Team: Toygar Bazarkaya, Stefan Meske (CD), Anneli Tomfort (AD), Constantin Sossidi (copy)

A brand of jewelry,
watches and
leather goods.

Ad for makeup: 'Make the
most of what you show.'

LINHA OX FACE.
VOCÊ QUE PODE SE MOSTRAR, APROVEITE.

OX

BATOM · GLOSS · LAPISEIRA DELINEADORA PARA OLHOS E LÁBIOS · SOMBRA EM LÁPIS
DELINEADOR LÍQUIDO · LÁPIS PARA OLHOS E LÁBIOS · MÁSCARA PARA CÍLIOS

SAC: 0800-121015
ox.cosmeticos@uol.com.br

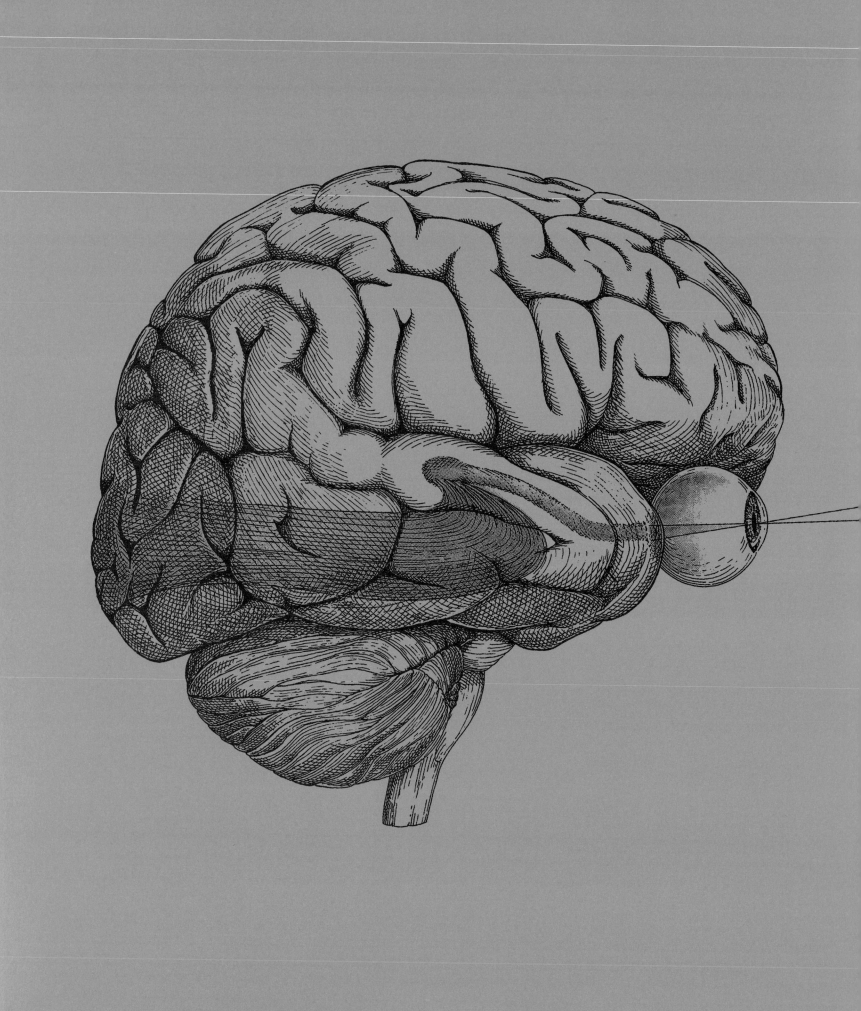

The first part of this
book deliberately leaves
out any explanations,
in order to let all those
fantastic ads work their
magic. One fascinating
thing about them is the
fact that each one works
quite spontaneously,
without us having any
previous experience or
background knowledge.
This chapter, however, is
an invitation to everyone
who would like to know

#11 FROM EYES TO BRAIN

more, and is curious
about what happens when
a visual trick has left the
eye and entered the brain.
After a brief survey of
current research on the
nature of perception in a
variety of disciplines, we
shall try to shed some
light on the optical
illusions used in the first
ten chapters. Take a look,
then, at what goes on
behind the seen.

SPOT THE DIFFERENCE!

You don't understand what you're supposed to do? You can't see a picture on the opposite page? That's because your perception is limited. In actual fact there is no difference between these two pictures: it's the same image being represented in different ways.

You can interpret one of them easily enough, and a computer can decipher the other, which is in hexadecimal code (a sixteen-digit representation of the colour of each pixel). We humans have learned to perceive images from dots of printer ink rather than numerical

codes. In the early 20th century, René Magritte challenged existing notions of perception through works such as *The Treachery of Images* (below). His statement, 'This is not a pipe', remains indisputable, for neither picture is a real pipe – just a representation.

WHAT DO THESE PICTURES HAVE IN COMMON?

Do you think that's an easy question? On both pages you can see a horse, or so you think. However, if you look more closely, you'll see that the two pictures have absolutely nothing in common. In the picture opposite you can see a few scribbles, a rough outline, and a subjective area in between. Below, you see surfaces with fine degrees of colour and brightness. Viewed in this way, there is nothing to indicate that you are looking at the same animal. Nevertheless, all of us without hesitation can identify a horse in both pictures. This introduction to the theoretical section of this book shows that perception is a complex as well as a fascinating process. It can be fun to look more closely into it, to try to understand it, and sometimes also to question what we think we see.

VISION AND PERCEPTION: A GENERAL OVERVIEW

The ability to see and visually construct is inborn. Virtually everybody can do it, regardless of IQ, financial status and social class. Seeing seems to us to be one of the simplest things in the world. This is not the case, however.

Perception is experience of our environment by means of all our senses together. These five senses were defined by Aristotle (384–322 BC) in his *De Anima* as sight, hearing, smell, taste and touch. We shall soon see that sight is not in first place by chance.

The human brain is predominantly devoted to sight. About fifty per cent of the cerebral cortex is used to analyse visual information.

Aristotle's definition stems from a very early phase of research into perception. More than 2,000 years later, psychologist Professor Philip Zimbardo of Stanford University described perception as follows:

'Perception is the ordering principle that gives coherence to kaleidoscopic sensory input and meaningful unity to separated elements, making possible an organized direction of our behavior. Without the organizing processes of perception, we would not see objects, space, events, movement, people, or relationships, but would drift through a world of meaningless, random sensations.' (Psychology and Life, *Glenview, IL, 1988*)

Here we have several new and highly relevant observations. Perception is a process of construction which actively creates order. It involves the absorption and processing of information and not just a pure image of the world around us.

Sight, which of course is responsible for the visual element of perception, has a central function in this process, but although its role is of vital importance, it is only one contributor to the overall process.

How, then, are we to define sight? One online attempt to do so runs as follows: 'The ability to receive light stimuli and to recognize and understand the information they contain about the world around us.... The process of seeing, particularly in the higher mammals and humans, is extremely complex. It begins with the optic image of the object on the retina, transforms these optic stimuli into nerve impulses and passes them on to the cerebral cortex, and it is here that the necessary process of awareness and recognition takes place. How these physiological processes are turned into recognition and comprehension as well as suitable courses of action remains for the most part a mystery.'

The way in which one of our most natural and most important faculties works 'remains a mystery'! This is certainly not due to any lack of interest on the part of scholars and scientists. On the contrary, there is no end to the research or the number of publications on the subject in many different disciplines, and on the pages that follow you will find a brief survey of the latest findings by biologists, physicists, psychologists, doctors and artists.

Although they are all hunting for answers, clearly many of the questions remain open. In any case, our study of their collective wisdom is of limited relevance to the subject of visual design.

We do not need to know what chemical reactions take place in the cones and rods of the retina in order to produce a good poster. Yet some findings – on the psychology of perception, for instance – can be applied directly to the daily tasks of the graphic designer and are extremely useful when it comes to answering the perennial question: 'How can I present my subject or product from a different angle?'

When scientists talk about sight, they generally mean the purely optical mechanics of receiving and processing visual signals. But when we talk about sight in an everyday context, we don't just mean the image of our environment on the retina. It is only through our interpretation of this information through a complex interaction with the brain that the eye's reception of something turns into proper sight or perception.

In what follows, we shall be talking a lot about perception, but as our concern is exclusively with the sense of sight, perception will always be meant in a visual sense.

The most important thing to bear in mind is the fact that seeing is not merely a matter of stimulus and reaction, as was long thought to be the case, but is a highly developed process of construction which we are only just beginning to understand.

Communications expert Professor Norbert Bolz has come up with an original but pertinent description of this process: 'Successful perception is a construct of which one can only say: the world has nothing against it!'

VISION IN SCIENCE AND NATURE

The natural philosopher and astronomer Johannes Kepler

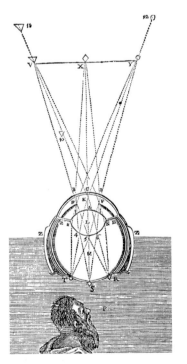

Drawing of how sight functions by René Descartes

Under the heading 'science' we shall include the views and findings of both biologists and physicists, as for the most part these overlap or complement one another. Both approach the subject from a technical standpoint, and are concerned with the optic, mechanical and – since the advent of neurology – chemical processes of perception.

The Greek philosophers of the school of Epicurus (341–270 BC) thought that objects radiated images of themselves in all directions, and these penetrated the eye, thus causing vision. The problem with this theory was soon apparent: if all objects projected images of themselves in all directions, the images would surely get mixed up and would interfere with one another. Besides, how could the images of large objects make their way through the tiny opening of the eye?

Plato (c. 429–347 BC) assumed that light emanated from the eye and joined up with sunlight to form a medium that connected up with the eye and facilitated sight. Similar approaches were made down through the centuries, and are to be found again in Euclid and Leonardo da Vinci. However, in 1492, da Vinci himself realized that there were problems with this so-called 'extramission theory'. It had now been discovered that light needed time to spread itself. For example, it would take over a month for the image to reach the eye if one wanted to see the sun.

The beginnings of modern optics are associated with Johannes Kepler (1571–1630). He was an astronomer and natural philosopher, and in defining rays of light he had already come up with the concept of waves, which he saw as a means of transport. Eventually, in 1604, he discovered that the function of the eye was to focus the image on the retina.

The 'blind spot' has been known since 1666, and is striking evidence of the constructional nature of sight. There is always one point in our field of vision where we cannot see anything. But thanks to our wonderful talent for constructing images, we are simply unaware of it, because we always fill in this gap with the missing information.

René Descartes (1596–1650) discovered the law of reflection – the angle of incidence equals the angle of reflection. He also defined light as a kind of pressure in a firm medium, and thus laid the foundations of the theory of light waves.

In the 17th century, there was a fierce dispute between the adherents of the wave theory and those of the particle theory of light. The Dutch astronomer and watchmaker Christiaan Huygens was the most popular wave theorist, and declared that light was movement within material and not transport of material.

Sir Isaac Newton, who in 1704 published *Opticks*, is regarded as the best-known of the particle theorists. He proved through experiments with glass prisms that white light was composed of a spectrum of colours from red to violet. He therefore assumed that light consisted of tiny particles into which it could be split.

Thomas Young (1773–1829) came up with the theory of interference (the overlapping effect when waves come together), and this proved to be the decisive argument in favour of the wave theory. Young even succeeded in determining the wavelengths of light: red 676 nanometres, violet 424 nanometres. The particle theory was therefore, for the time being at least, discredited.

In the second half of the 19th century, it was discovered that light and electricity were connected, and that the visual element of light was only one small part of the spectrum of electromagnetic waves.

The wave theory of light came back into the reckoning after the discovery of photons (quanta of visible light), and current research confirms that these have the qualities both of waves and of particles. Hence the key concept of wave-particle duality.

This groundwork in the field of physics is important for our understanding of the way sight works in humans and animals. As Newton already made clear in his *Opticks*, rays of light themselves are not coloured. The colours are produced by our nervous system when this is stimulated by a particular wavelength of light. But the link between wavelength and perception could also be quite different.

There is nothing inherently red in long-wave light, any more than blue is inherent in short-wave light. The idea that these familiar perceptions are only constructed may be more easily understood if we discuss what animals see.

There are many examples which prove that animals perceive forms of energy humans cannot register. Bees, for instance, can perceive ultraviolet light, but we have absolutely no idea what 'colour' they see it as. Their nervous system produces a sensitivity to colour which is very distinct from our own, even with wavelengths that we can also perceive. All we know for sure is that their sensitivity to these very short wavelengths enables bees to find and distinguish between different kinds of flowers. They are also orientated by the sun, even when this has disappeared behind the clouds. To do this, they use the polarization of UV light in patches of blue sky.

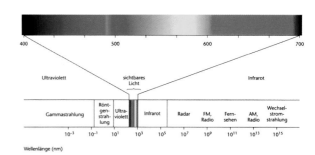

First row, from left to right: ultraviolet, visible light, infrared. Second row: gamma ray, X-ray, ultraviolet, infrared, radar, FM radio, television, AM radio, alternating current. Final row: wavelength (in nanometres). Within the overall spectrum of waves, it is clear how narrow the range is within which all our visual perception takes place.

Drawing by Leonardo da Vinci

Experiment 1

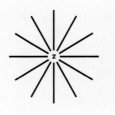

Experiment 2

Two experiments to help you find your blind spot. Close your right eye and look at the cross with your left eye. If you are at the right distance, the black spot will disappear in Experiment 1, and in Experiment 2 you will see a star that is completed in the centre.

The ability of honeybees to perceive UV light helps them to find various types of flower.

Ripe fruit reflects more UV light than unripe fruit.

The proverbial eagle eye not only sees sharply but can also perceive UV light, which helps it in its search for prey.

Many birds also have the ability to see UV light. In their search for a partner, a pattern in the feathers is very important, though this is invisible to the human eye. Ripe fruits and berries reflect a great deal of UV light and that is why animals can pick them out at once. The fact that mouse urine gives off an ultraviolet glow helps birds of prey to hunt them even from a great height.

The praying mantis can locate a fly with the help of its binocular vision. When the fly is within reach, it flicks out its front leg and grabs its prey at the point where the head joins the body.

Mantis shrimp have ten colour receptors and determine distances with just one eye, while bats use ultrasound to find their way around. The density of cones in the retinas of eagles and falcons is two to three times greater than in humans, which explains their sharpness of vision.

It is thought that doves have pentachromatic perception (i.e. based on five colours), whereas humans are usually trichromatic (three). Our receptors respond to the colours red, green and blue, which we combine to make all other colours, including black and white. Colour blindness is caused by people seeing dichromatically (two basic colours), so that what they perceive is reduced. This means that a creature with five types of colour receptor, like the dove, sees a greater spectrum of colours than us humans. Unfortunately, there is no way that we can conceive what this 'greater spectrum' might consist of.

Some humans are also tetrachromats (four colours), although this ability is only found in women. These people have an additional type of cone which is sensitive to yellows and enables them to have a far more refined sense of colour than most people. Tetrachromats can perceive images where the rest of us can only see a yellow surface.

All these different levels of perception have one thing in common: in all living creatures, sight is a constructive process. The equipment that is used varies as it is adapted to the special needs of the individual species.

A good example of this is the Tinbergen experiment illustrated at the top of page 209. Nikolaas Tinbergen (1907–88), a Dutch ethologist and ornithologist, shared the Nobel Prize in Physiology or Medicine in 1973 for his work on behaviour patterns in animals. What is particularly fascinating about the experiment shown here is that even the simplest forms can trigger off imaginative constructions and related reactions. Such reactions may well be of vital importance for an animal's survival.

The position and direction of the eyes are also adapted in different creatures according to their specific needs. Humans, cats and dogs, for example, have a good perception of spatial depth as their eyes face forwards and the field of vision from each eye overlaps. Animals that have eyes on the side of their heads, such as horses, fish or birds, have a more panoramic view. Many of these creatures are even able to focus their eyes independently of one other, whereas eyes that focus forwards can only move together and focus on one thing at a time.

Turning our attention back to humans, it is important to look at how the sense of sight develops. At just one month, babies blink when an object moves towards their eyes. At the age of three months, they can perceive the outlines of objects, and at four months they can make out three-dimensional forms. Through awareness of shading, perspective and intermediate positions, at seven months they are able to construct the depth, position and shape of an object. By the time they are one year old, the visual faculty is already fully developed. Yet many children of this age have not yet learned to walk!

As many people are familiar with the way in which visual signals are processed, the explanation here shall remain brief. The iris, which opens and closes rather like the shutter of a camera, regulates the amount of light that enters the eye. This light falls on the lens, which curves and thereby regulates the focus. This is what enables us to decide on the distance at which we wish to see something clearly.

Everyone must have seen home movies that are blurred because the camera held to the eye follows every movement of the person making the film. That, in effect, is how we see everything all the time. Why, then, doesn't the world around us appear blurred?

We don't continuously see one overall picture, as a video camera does, but are constantly putting pictures together piece by piece. Because this happens so quickly, we don't realize what we are doing. To us it seems that we are seeing the whole page of this book and maybe also the table on which it is lying. If, however, we pay close attention, and focus on a single word in this text, we will not even be able to identify a word standing two lines above it. In order to do that, we would have to move our eyes again. By moving our eyes, we bring the image of what we want to see into the so-called 'yellow spot' (macula). This is part of the fovea centralis – the point in the retina where vision is at its sharpest.

In the retina there are extremely sensitive rod cells which work even in the faintest light. They measure the light coming in and deliver an image of the surroundings in different shades of grey. The less sensitive cone cells are for colour vision and for seeing in bright light. The almost inconceivable quantity of rods (around 120 million) and cones (around 7 million) work constantly to translate the light information received into electrical impulses. These, in turn, are transmitted through the optic nerve into the brain.

This is where the active process of visual construction begins, through which the impulses are transformed by the brain into what we generally call 'sight'. Despite all the efforts of scientists the world over, we are still only in the early stages of research into this amazing process.

Tinbergen experiment: Chickens and ducks identify the cardboard cross on the left as a harmless goose, and the one on the right as a falcon, which makes them take flight.

Animals that are constantly on the look-out for enemies have their eyes at the side, thus increasing their field of vision. The eyes of a predator are at the front, giving it better perception of depth.

VISION AND PSYCHOLOGY

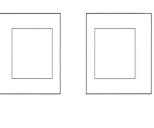

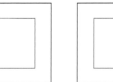

Stereoscopic vision.
Put a piece of paper as
a 'partition' between the
figures, and hold your head
so close to the paper that
your right eye can only see
the right-hand picture, and
your left eye the left-hand
picture. You will see the red
square hovering in front of
the black one at the top,
and behind it at the bottom.

A still from the Lumière
brothers' film *The Arrival of
a Train at La Ciotat Station*
(1895)

'The illusion that perception is a simple process follows from the ease with which we perceive. The reality, however, is that perception is the outcome of an extraordinary process that is accomplished by mechanisms which, in their exquisite complexity, work so well that the outcome – our awareness of the environment and our ability to navigate through it – occurs effortlessly under most conditions.' (E. Bruce Goldstein, Blackwell's Handbook of Perception, *Oxford, 2001*)

The history of the psychology of perception began with some experiments in the second half of the 19th century. The aim was to break down the complexities of the process into simple tasks, and then to identify which external stimuli led to which perceptual responses. These experiments gave us the first insights into elementary processes such as the perception of colour, movement and space.

Similar experiments were conducted with the other senses, such as hearing. The hope was that progressive study would lead automatically from explanations of simple processes to more complex ones, but this didn't happen.

The right eye and the left eye, because of their distance from one another, deliver slightly different images to their respective retinas. This observation led British physicist Charles Wheatstone (1802–75) to construct one of the first stereoscopes. Using this apparatus, it is possible to create a convincing impression of depth with the aid of two slightly different pictures. Among other things, this principle was used for the 3-D films that were so popular during the 1950s.

On 23 December 1895, the Lumière Brothers showed one of the first films in a Parisian café, with the thrilling title: *The Arrival of a Train at La Ciotat*. The sight of a train apparently entering the room caused such a panic among the audience that they fell over themselves trying to get out of the way, and proceeded to run outside. In those days, the film didn't even have any sound. Today we would need the most sophisticated 3-D technology with moving chairs and rushing air in order to create a similar illusion.

It is scarcely surprising to hear the reports of anthropologists about primitive peoples who have never seen a photograph before. Apparently they weigh the photograph in their hands, turn it around, and simply do not know what to do with it. When it is explained to them that it shows a person they know, they begin to understand and from that moment on are able to 'read' photographs.

At noon one day in 1896, the psychologist George W. Stratton began an experiment in which for one week he wore a spectacle-like device that inverted top and bottom, and left and right, through the use of prisms. In this way, he proved that the body adapts itself to the visual system. He began to adjust to his new perceptions and to change the connections he was making. Initially he found it irritating that sounds seemed to come from the opposite direction to where the object was situated, but after just a few days he found that he would hear something from the right and automatically turn left.

The Russian filmmaker Lev Kuleshov (1899–1970) amazed everyone with an experiment in 1923. In various sequences, he filmed a close-up of a man who seemed completely expressionless, and he tested it on an invited audience. Depending on which scenes he screened before showing them the expressionless man, the spectators came up with totally different interpretations of the situation. They automatically established a connection between those scenes and the man. For instance, after a shot of a bowl of soup, they thought the man looked hungry; after a corpse, they thought he looked sad; and after a naked woman, he was seen as lustful.

During the 1950s, a large-scale repetition of Stratton's prism experiment attracted a great deal of attention. In the 'Innsbruck spectacles experiment', the human guinea pigs were asked to wear prism glasses for up to 124 days, with top and bottom, and left and right once again reversed. These massive disturbances to the perception system were resolved by the brain after a short period of adjustment, and the volunteers were then able to go back into the outside world as if nothing had happened. After a few weeks, they could ride their motorbikes through Innsbruck, play tennis and go skiing. Even reading back to front proved no problem. After they had discarded the apparatus, it took just a few minutes for them to adjust back to the normal order of things. The experiment showed that human perception is extremely adaptable and swift to learn new tricks.

I was able to make a similar observation when I was a student. When you're sitting at the computer, just try to turn the mouse 180 degrees and work with it. You'll undoubtedly fail because the cursor will always move in the opposite direction to the mouse. I was therefore all the more surprised when one day I saw a fellow student quite naturally working with the mouse the wrong way round. Her explanation: the first time she used a mouse, she thought, quite logically, that its tail (the cable) should be behind it! The fact that she could work just as easily with this technique as anyone else shows just how well our perceptions can adapt.

At around the time of the Innsbruck experiment, American psychologist James J. Gibson

George W. Stratton, whose experiments with prisms turned the world upside down

Kuleshov's experiment. According to the combination of film sequences, people attributed totally different emotions to the man in the second picture.

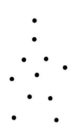

Gunnar Johansson's experiments showed that it was possible to identify the way a person was moving with just eleven spots.

(1904–79) developed a theory that went directly against all current opinions. Natural perception was the focal point of his analysis. In his view, the study of sight should begin not with the image on the retina but with the motive for action. In other words, perception was not a neutral process but was governed by functional factors related to the underlying purpose.

Another of Gibson's findings was related to active observation. He spoke of the active acquisition of specific information as the key feature of sight. It was not a matter simply of 'having' visual impressions that were enforced from outside and passively accepted by the system.

A third vital point concerned the way that perception can be trained – for example among people working on a production line and watching out for faults. After a while, this could be done quickly, automatically and very accurately.

In 1950, Gunnar Johansson began his experiments on motion perception. He used film sequences of movements, in which the people themselves were not visible: it was only possible to see bright spots from lights that had been fixed to the relevant parts of the body. His results proved that our perception system, using nothing but the patterns of movement reproduced on film, is able to quickly and effortlessly construct the type of movement shown.

In 1956, Béla Julesz (1928–2003) began to research binocular vision. By experimenting with computer-generated stereograms in which two slightly staggered images were combined with a random pattern, he proved that three-dimensional stereovision must begin at a very early stage of information processing: even without visible shading, outlines and other indicative features, we can clearly see three-dimensional images within the random patterns. From 1989, Julesz was head of the Visual Perception Research Department at Bell Laboratories, New Jersey.

In 1979, the psychologist Ulric Neisser (b. 1928) identified another factor. He was interested in the role of memory in perception, and he theorized that perception is not possible without memory, which actively imposes an order on the knowledge we acquire. Only through memory is it possible to interpret the information we receive. Our personal 'data bank' is therefore constantly being expanded through existing information and new experiences.

Since the 1980s, research into perception has been a specific field of neurology. Scientists analyse the

Autostereograms only became possible through Julesz's discoveries. Allow your gaze to wander into the distance as you look at this pattern, and you will see the cube.

neuron activities of the brain during the processing of information. The hope is to gain insight into our cognitive abilities as well as knowledge that might be used to solve the many technical problems of developing artificial intelligence.

Even today, the psychology of perception is an area with many blank spots, but we have also gleaned a great deal of knowledge, together with some rules that merit a closer look. Many are generally if not universally valid, some influence one another, while others are mutually exclusive. There are no either/or definitions, but they all work through probabilities.

We are not taught these rules; we simply learn them from the visual experiences to which we are constantly exposed from earliest childhood. Through these rules, we are later able to understand images that we have never seen before.

In relation to signal processing, author Donald D. Hoffman coined the term 'visual intelligence' in his book of that title. It is very much to the point, because there is no learning by rote of limitless forms and objects; instead, what we all possess is a 'handbook of seeing'.

Familiar visual impressions play an important role. This is clear from the fact that different cultures have different senses of perception. The ancient Egyptians would certainly not have found their typical profile portraits as strange as we do.

A modern example is the stereotypical modes of representation in comic books. Particular graphic techniques are employed to convey movement, speed and other special effects. We learn very quickly to decipher this sort of representation.

To Europeans, Asians may look much more like each other than we do, and vice versa. It can take years for us to learn to distinguish between people from a different ethnic background. The same applies to telling identical twins apart. It may seem impossible to outsiders, but family members have no trouble at all.

One might conclude that perception is a feeling moulded by subjective experience. This is illustrated with the sense of taste. Exactly the same input – for example, celery – can elicit totally opposite sensory impressions in different people. Why, then, should there not be the same degree of variation in sight as there is in taste?

This relief in the temple of Kom Ombo shows the typical profile portrait found in ancient Egyptian culture.

The manner in which movement is depicted in comic strips has to be learned culturally.

Outsiders find it almost impossible to distinguish between identical twins, but close family members have no difficulty. (Photograph by Ratiopharm, which uses twins to advertise its generic medicines.)

VISION AND THE MEDICAL WORLD

Medicine is a very interesting area in the study of sight, because when it deals with vision-related conditions, it examines what happens when this highly complex and delicate system goes wrong. We shall now take a look at certain illnesses – some of them very rare – that enhance our understanding of the seeing process.

Neurologists Frank Benson and John Greenberg reported on a patient who after carbon monoxide poisoning suffered from 'optic agnosia'. This meant that most areas of his visual faculties remained intact (sharpness of vision, colours, detection of motion), but he was incapable of combining what he saw into recognizable people or objects.

The result was dramatic. He could remember what people and objects looked like, but the only way he could recognize them was by way of familiar sounds or voices. His ability to bring the various pieces of visual information into meaningful order had been destroyed – yet more proof that we have to visually construct the objects we 'see'.

Hallucinations do the very opposite. The hallucinator cannot stop constructing images. This is the problem for patients suffering, for instance, from Charles Bonnet Syndrome: they see imaginary people, animals, buildings and even complex landscapes as if these were actually there, and are unable to distinguish between their illusions and the real world. They only become aware of their mistake when someone else points it out.

Everyone can have a similar experience any night of the year. When we dream, we also construct realistic or possibly surrealistic scenes and situations in all their complexity.

In 1728, the surgeon William Cheselden (1688–1752) reported on an operation in which artificial pupils were inserted into the eye of a 13-year-old boy to relieve him from cataracts. The boy had never been able to see anything before the operation. After it, he was unable to judge distances properly. It seemed to him as if every object was going to 'touch his eyes' in the same way as it would touch the skin when handled.

Two months after the operation, the boy saw objects in pictures as three-dimensional rather than two-dimensional coloured surfaces. To his amazement, however, he found that the images did not feel like objects when he touched them. He then wondered which was lying – his sense of sight or his sense of touch.

This operation offered the first answer to a question posed by the Irish philosopher William Molyneux (1656–98). In a letter to his fellow philosopher John Locke, he wrote:

A Man, being born blind, and having a Globe and a Cube, nigh of the same bigness, Committed into his Hands, and being taught or Told, which is Called the Globe, and which the Cube, so as easily to distinguish them by his Touch or Feeling; Then both being taken from Him, and Laid on a Table, Let us Suppose his Sight Restored to Him; Whether he Could, by his Sight, and before he touch them, know which is the Globe and which the Cube?

This intriguing question preoccupied European philosophers during the 18th century. After Cheselden's operation, clearly the answer had to be no. This may be hard to conceive, but it is essential to bear in mind that, for the 13-year-old boy, there was absolutely no correspondence between what he saw and what he touched.

This concept might be easier to grasp if you imagine someone being cured of severe colour blindness and suddenly being able to see things in colour instead of in black and white. How would the patient know which of the shades he had seen before now corresponded to green, red or yellow?

A rare affliction that may follow on from a stroke illustrates the fact that perception of movement too is a process of construction. A woman complained that she was completely unable to see movement, although her perception of depth and objects as well as her sharpness of vision were quite unaffected. People and objects suddenly appeared out of the blue. Movements, such as liquid being poured into a glass, looked like a sculpture to her. This form of defective vision can be simulated in healthy people by applying strong magnetic fields to particular areas of the brain.

Synaesthesia is not regarded as a disease but as a neuropsychological condition. It is hereditary and occurs six times more frequently in women than in men. Sufferers experience several sense perceptions at the same time: they see colours and shapes when they hear music or when they smell a scent. In their mind's eye, numbers appear in a particular colour.

With synaesthesia, the link between sense stimuli and visual perception is the most common, but theoretically it can affect all five senses. In other words, one can smell sounds, touch smells, or taste sights. This phenomenon has been known for centuries, but it is still a mystery. What is clear, however, is that the stimulus can affect several senses, and this is borne out by tests that show two separate areas of the brain becoming active at the same time. How and why this simultaneity occurs are questions that have not yet been answered.

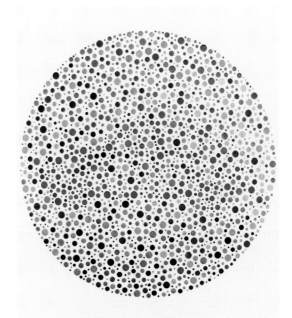

Wenn Sie den VW nicht sehen, können Sie kein VW-Inspekteur werden.

'If you can't see the VW, you will never be a VW inspector.' The principle behind this VW advert from 1964 is used in tests for colour blindness. The copy accompanying the advert continues: 'We can't shut our eyes to these things. Before we allow our testers to test a VW, we test them. Their eyes, their hearts and their kidneys.'

VISION AND ART

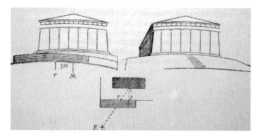

Sketch of the Acropolis and its perspective layout by Le Corbusier.

Hugo van der Goes, *The Birth of Christ*: In this painting, important figures are depicted larger than the rest, regardless of natural perspective.

The active process of seeing is clearly basic to the observation of art. If it wasn't, we would only see blobs of colour on a canvas or on photographic paper, and at the cinema we would be looking at coloured lights on a white wall. There would be no trace of peeled fruit, sunsets, battle scenes or tear-jerking love stories. For us to be able to see all these things, painters, photographers or film directors must know how to capture the subject in their chosen medium. The skill of the painter lies in organizing the blobs of colour in such a way that the visual faculties of the observer can either construct an image or, in the case of a Cubist painting, for instance, be deliberately disorientated.

Many scientific discoveries are surprisingly relevant to the field of art. It is important to know how perception of depth functions if a work is to appear three-dimensional. As a painter knows that with two eyes he can see things in three dimensions, he may well close one eye in order to gain more control over the way he transfers reality onto his two-dimensional canvas.

Knowledge of perspective and constants is important for the spatial layout of paintings. The Romans already knew about the use of perspective to represent three dimensions: in Pompeii, frescoes were found depicting a painted garden which seemed to be a continuation of a room.

Architecture is another field in which visual weaknesses play a role. In Ancient Greece, knowledge of perspective was also incorporated into the planning of buildings. That is why some columns are broader at the top, so that from the standpoint of the observer they seem to be completely straight. The distances between the columns of the Acropolis are not identical: they are arranged in such a way that from a particular angle they will appear to be equally spaced. Le Corbusier analysed this in his treatise *Vers une architecture* (1925), and regarded the Pantheon as the pinnacle of all architecture.

During the centuries that followed, this knowledge wasn't developed any further. In early Christian and medieval painting, the size of the people and objects depicted was almost exclusively determined by their status rather than their spatial position. Instead, overlapping or scenic effects were used to indicate space.

Central perspective was rediscovered during the Renaissance, and 'painter architects' such as Filippo Brunelleschi, Leon Battista Alberti and Giotto di Bondone depicted themes from Christian iconography in architectural settings that were accurately constructed.

In 1525, Albrecht Dürer (1471–1528) published his book *Underweysung der messung mit dem zirckel un richtscheyt*, which was the first account of mathematical process relating to perspective, and provides the basis for geometrical representation.

In order to cope with the problem of size and perspective, artists use various methods. Holding the brush or pencil with outstretched hand often helps to make comparative measurements, in order to establish the 'real' size. It can also be useful to look at scenes through a grid. In recent times, photographs have also been used as an aid – Heinrich Zille, Max Liebermann and René Magritte are among the artists who are known to have used photographs as models for their paintings.

Knowledge of perspective has played a special role in the so-called 'trompe-l'œil' style. In this illusionistic manner of painting, the artist attempts as realistically as possible to remove the boundaries between picture and reality. There are wonderful examples of such work on the ceilings of many churches. Looking

up from a particular standpoint, it is often not possible to distinguish where the architecture ends and the painting begins. Such paintings often serve to make the building seem bigger than it is.

In the late 19th century and throughout the 20th century the world of the artist was 'seen' in radically different ways.

Impressionism (*c.* 1860–1905)

The aim of the Impressionists was to reproduce individual moods and sensual impressions of colour, space and light. Outlines disappear behind structures, and the pictures seem unresolved, even blurred, thus leaving room for one's own projections. Artists such as Claude Monet, Pierre-Auguste Renoir, Camille Pissarro, Frédéric Bazille and Alfred Sisley shaped this particular style.

Expressionism (*c.* 1905–1920)

In Expressionism, strong colours and emphatic outlines distorted reality for emotional effect. Little attention was paid to the elaboration of details. By comparison with earlier forms of painting, these largely angst-ridden forms of expression represented a genuine revolution in the manner in which things were 'seen'. The original strokes with which the artist applied the paint now became an integral part of the composition. The best-known Expressionists include Paul Gauguin, Erich Heckel, Emil Nolde, Franz Marc, Paul Klee and Wassily Kandinsky.

Surrealism (*c.* 1920–70)

With the Surrealists, dream and reality merged. These artists placed realistic objects in fantastic contexts, so that visual perception based on knowledge of the laws of

In Albrecht Dürer's *The Lute*, we see an artist with a frame and a thread, which he uses as an aid to establish the correct perspective for his painting of the musical instrument.

The perspective of many ceiling frescoes is so accurate that it is difficult to distinguish between the architecture and the painting.

A Surrealist painting by René Magritte: *Carte Blanche* (1965)

Sketch of *Head Mounted Display* by Alfons Schilling

Schilling's 'Perceptual Machines' always provide an experience for the whole body.

With this prismatic construction on a hill in New York, Alfons Schilling provided a view over the Hudson such as might be seen by a giant with an interocular distance of five metres.

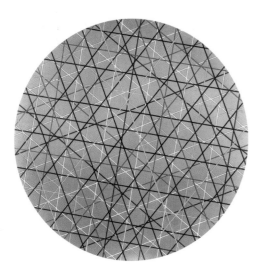

Richard Kriesche, 1966

nature was disturbed and thrown into doubt. Famous representatives of this style included Salvador Dalí, Giorgio de Chirico, René Magritte, André Breton and Max Ernst.

The Modern Age (from *c.* 1970)

In the 20th and early 21st centuries, art has become an equal partner in our study of perception. Many artists demand active participation from the observer to complete or experience their work. In this respect, art can be seen as a kind of productive research, in the sense that these works enable us to gain a better understanding of the processes that take place inside our brains.

As examples of the many different ways in which modern artists handle vision in their art, a few outstanding personalities deserve a mention. Most were represented at the exhibition 'Einbildung' ['Imagination'] at the Kunsthaus, Graz in December 2003.

Since the 1960s, Alfons Schilling has been experimenting with all kinds of media to explore the subject of perception. With one experimental installation after another, he uses the processes of vision as the basis of his art. It all began in 1968, when a kitschy 3-D postcard came into his possession. The technique fascinated him, and he began to engage in photographic experiments and delve deeper into the subject of stereovision. In 1973, he described and sketched a contraption with two small monitors in front of the eyes (see top left). This apparatus was one of the earliest precursors of cyberspace and virtual reality.

In the course of his intensive work on stereograms and his

construction of various pieces of machinery to enable observation of these pictures, in the mid 1970s Schilling began to build so-called 'seeing machines' which radically changed the way people viewed things and enabled them to see the world through completely different eyes. These pieces of equipment do not just change the view by means of prisms (as was the case with Stratton's experiments described on page 211), but because of their size and mode of operation, they provide a new experience for the whole body.

In the 1960s, Richard Kriesche created systems that divided pictures up into elements. This caused the observer to perceive spatial depth in a constant state of flux.

Gianni Colombo (1937–93) first exhibited his *Elastic Space* at the much acclaimed show 'Trigon '67' in Graz. The following year he presented it at the Venice Biennale and at Documenta IV in Kassel. A cubic grid made from nylon threads was stretched out in a pitch-dark room with an irregularly sloping floor; the threads were made visible with black light. The pattern of the threads was altered mechanically, so that the room was constantly changing. In such an unnatural environment, perception becomes so disorientated that visitors can easily lose their balance.

Colombo was a member of MID (Movimento Imagine Dimensione), an Italian group of artists and designers. They were influenced by a combination of architecture, art and design. Their works, in which movement always plays an important role, are installations in which the perception of the observer becomes a variable element in the experiment. Many of these installations are an invitation to interact as well as to experiment with one's own faculties of perception.

The work of the British op artist Bridget Riley (b. 1931), illustrated on page 227, is reminiscent of experimental, perceptual tests. The leitmotif of her paintings is her use of colour and its destabilizing effect. These large-scale pictures are a direct challenge to our sense of structure, and to an observer many of them look like they are actually moving or take on a three-dimensional appearance.

In the late 1960s, the work of the American artist Chuck Close (b. 1940) attracted a lot of attention. He sets out to 'translate' a photograph as perfectly as possibly into a painting, with a focus on the process of emergence. Like a scanner, he goes over the original, line by line, searching for the best painterly equivalent. He regards himself as a kind of interpreter, mediating between the language of photography and that of painting. He does this with virtually every technique available, from airbrush to watercolour to offset printing.

Manfred Willmann (b. 1952) also works with photographs. In 1976, he published his series of *Kontaktportraits*, which burst the frontiers of the medium. If we ignore the technical difficulties involved, the aim is 'simply' to break a picture up into segments, which our visual system then puts together again as a whole.

The same process is to be found in a work (1999) by Sarah Morris (b. 1967), which shows just how

powerful our perception of faces really is. Even in these solidly rectangular segments of colour, we can still make out the features of a face.

We should also not forget those artists who work with so-called 'impossible objects'. The first was Oscar Reutersvärd (1915–2002), who created the first 'impossible triangle' in 1934 (see page 231), and by 1986 had drawn approximately 2,500 of these impossible objects.

In 1958, Roger Penrose (b. 1931) published a picture of the impossible triangle (also known as the Penrose triangle), but said that it was not until 1984 that he had heard of Reutersvärd's drawings. Another representative of this style is Sandro del Prete.

M. C. Escher (1898–1972), who created the 'impossible cube' in 1958, is probably the best-known artist of this genre, although in fact he only published four pictures of impossible objects. The remainder of his work involves many sophisticated illusions using figure and ground.

Chuck Close, 1972

Manfred Willmann, 1976/1996

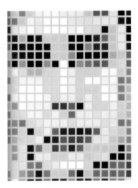

Sarah Morris, 1999

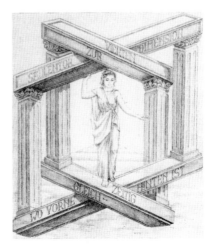

Sandro del Prete, *Gateway to the Fourth Dimension*

SEEING DEPENDS ON YOUR POINT OF VIEW

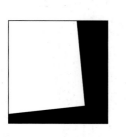

Above is the white subject, and below is the black.

Marcel Duchamp

We often 'see things differently' from someone else. Or we 'look at things from another perspective', or we have a 'point of view'. These expressions are now common turns of phrase, but all of them originate from the visual world, and with good reason.

How do we know what we ought to be seeing? Every time we open our eyes, we have a problem. Our field of vision is filled with information, all of which is of equal objective importance. We must therefore have certain criteria for deciding which is the subject and which is the background. This is an active process which we carry out continuously, even though most of the time we do it unconsciously.

We feel that we simply see the world as it is. That, however, is an insult to our perceptual system, because it is this system that makes things into what we see. But the processing of visual information has become so much a matter of routine that we scarcely even think about how complex it is, and we rarely bother to ask whether there might be other ways of seeing.

The first and most important of the processes is the division into figure and ground. We have to find borderlines that will separate the subject from the background. This is one of the most complex elements of perception, as can be gauged from the fact that despite massive investment, there is still no technology that can enable a computer to 'see' even remotely like a human being.

The division into figure and ground is vital, because it separates the important from the unimportant. Hearing involves a similar process, because we deliberately assign different levels of importance to what we hear. If, for example, we are sitting in a lively street café, we try to shut out every sound except our partner's voice. The rest becomes background noise.

Researchers have long been seeking the criteria used in the figure-versus-ground decision-making process, but no one has yet come up with the definitive answer. What we do have are common features – rather than rules – and to add to the complications, these frequently influence one another.

Is a zebra a white animal with black stripes?

Or a black animal with white stripes?

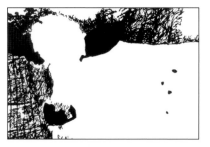

That two curves should happen by pure chance to run precisely parallel to one another is more than unlikely. This is why we see them as the outlines of shapes, the left being black and the right being white.

In Dallenbach's picture, without prior knowledge it is impossible to tell which is figure and which is ground. The solution is on page 269.

With this picture, it should be less difficult to interpret the subject.

When actively selecting, we only accept the most likely of the various competing images, and this process follows the same course in all of us.

Characteristic features of figure and ground:
• The figure seems more present than the background.
• The figure is seen as being in front of the background.
• The background appears amorphous.
• Lines and surfaces that divide figure and ground always belong to the figure.

We perceive figures when the relevant section of the image
• has a precise shape
• is meaningful
• tends to have a convex edge
• contains a concentration of smaller areas
• has matching colour components
• is clearly lit
• points in a vertical or horizontal direction
• is symmetrical or contains figures that relate to one another in a manner that is not random.

Take a look now at the pair of illustrations top left. Straight away, you will see the border lines, note the parallels and, independently of the colours between the parallel curves, define the figures. This is the principle of 'non-accidental' properties, as described by the psychologists Andrew Witkin and Marty Tenenbaum. We see a clear pattern, because it is extremely unlikely that two curves in a space could be situated in a 'non-accidental' relationship to one another and yet not be part of a subject.

However, the division into figure and ground doesn't always work

immediately. Psychologists in particular have devised many examples which quite deliberately cause problems for our faculties of perception.

When we look at the Dallenbach image, for instance, our visual system struggles to work out a meaningful, and hence stable interpretation of the black and white areas. We can actually feel our brain working as it tries to project familiar figures and combinations onto what we see.

But we shall be unsuccessful. Dallenbach spent a good deal of time searching for an image which would be impossible to interpret without prior knowledge. But once you have seen the solution, you will for the rest of your life be able to 'see' the image immediately – should you ever stumble across it again in another book.

Our reaction to the illustration below is similar. Our visual system gets to work at once, eager to establish a meaningful order. We are not satisfied with seeing a collection of black blobs. Only when we have made out the rider on horseback do we stop looking for other possible interpretations.

With the picture bottom left, the eye wanders aimlessly for a while in search of a meaningful context that will bring all the elements together. We know that we feel uneasy, and this feeling is only dissipated when we have seen the dalmatian. (If you are still having difficulty, hold the picture away from you.)

Once we have found a satisfactory interpretation, we seem to store the figure away. Later we shall have no trouble seeing the rider or the dog, but we will never perceive the picture again as we saw it first time – or at least not for a long time.

Picture puzzles offer different problems in the separation of figure and ground. In this case, however, we are not destabilized because we cannot find a clear meaning. Here it is the exact opposite: we can find too many possible meanings. As soon as we have fixed on one, the rest of the picture becomes background, but then suddenly it switches, and figure and ground change places.

Because of this constantly shifting ambiguity, we can have two or more possible interpretations of the same picture, which makes things difficult for us. When there is more than one meaning, our perception tries to settle on one, because it can never deliver a mixture of meanings. The different elements can be seen either exclusively as figure or exclusively as ground, but not both at the same time.

These two-way pictures were known as long ago as 1795. Above right, we can see what may well be the oldest known example, the so-called 'Rubin Cup'. It was so famous that it spawned many imitations, but it was not until 200 years later that psychologists began to take an interest in ambivalence of this type.

How do we actually proceed when we want to see what we're supposed to? Once we have found an outline, we separate the picture into segments. With the cup, as with all such pictures, we look for the borders of these segments at the points where the curve is at its greatest. These are indicated in the

second diagram. Switching the focus also brings about a switch in the borders of the segments. Experiments have shown that it is possible to influence which variations are given preference. If the curve of the facial features were accentuated, more people would see the face first – and vice versa.

It is not only scientists that have discovered this technique – artists too are fascinated by it. Peter Jenny has magically turned the 'nothing' between two objects into a 'genuine' Picasso. A vase that was presented to Queen Elizabeth II on her Silver Jubilee shows her and her husband in profile.

The drawing bottom right is a rather more elaborate trick. It uses the same principle as the 'Rubin Cup', but misleads us. So long as we keep trying to see two faces, one on either side of the candle holder, we feel uneasy. Something is not right. Only when we can see a single face behind the stick, as opposed to two profiles, does the image become stable.

William Turton, title page of *A Conchological Dictionary of the British Islands*, 1819

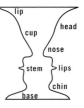

The Rubin Cup with its segments identified

Extract from Picasso's *Guernica* and two objects by Peter Jenny

This vase with profiles of Queen Elizabeth II and the Duke of Edinburgh was created for the Queen's Silver Jubilee in 1977.

Roger N. Shepard, *Egyptian-Eyezed Tête-à-Tête*

M. C. Escher, *Mosaic II*, 1957

Roger N. Shepard, *The Attractive Balustrade*, published in the *Stanford Magazine* (1984)

Sandro del Prete, *The Window Opposite*

Yin-Yang symbol, *c.* 700–1000 BC

Clockwise from top left: Alaska SeaLife Center, Mikal Kellner Foundation (for the protection of animals), a recycling centre and Sacramento Zoo

M. C. Escher, who once said, 'I could fill a whole second life working on my pictures,' spent fifty years playing almost exclusively with the principle of figure and ground. The picture at the top of page 224 is one such work. There is not a single section that could not be a figure.

Roger N. Shepard, describing the drawing immediately below the M. C. Escher picture, writes that the word figure takes on a very special meaning here. A similar row of lifesize three-dimensional columns was constructed by David Barker for the Exploratorium Museum of Science, San Francisco.

The Swiss artist Sandro del Prete is another who specializes in optical illusions and impossible objects. The picture in the centre shows a plant, a cat on the window ledge, washing on the line, a curtain, a glass and a shelf. Or can you see something else?

Freelance artists are not the only ones to enjoy switching figure and ground. The technique also offers graphic designers an opportunity to come up with more exciting logos. Probably the oldest, most famous and most copied two-way picture is the yin-yang symbol, and we must certainly give it full credit for its role as forerunner of all logo designs. You can see some more recent logos bottom left. Animals seem to be particularly suitable for designs like these.

Another form of picture puzzle is to be seen on the opposite page. Strictly speaking, this is not a switch between figure and ground, but the impression we get when looking at it may change from one moment to the next, giving it a completely new meaning. This occurs when we reorganize the visual information and attribute different meanings to the individual segments of the picture.

In the well-known drawing, *My Wife and My Mother-in-Law*, by W. E. Hill, the same section of the image represents the chin of the young woman and the nose of the old woman. A response to this drawing came from Jack Botwinick, who used a similar style to portray a young man and an old man. What works with two must work with three, thought a psychologist, who came up with a drawing containing three faces.

Why, especially when we feel dissatisfied with the figure we have found, we suddenly begin to construct another, is one of the many mysteries which – despite innumerable theories – no one has yet been able to solve. When we see one of these ambiguous figures for the first time, it presumably depends on chance as to which interpretation gets precedence. The spot on which the eyes focus first may be one of several factors that influence the decision. Once we have formed a stable and convincing image, we will stick to it initially.

This, however, is where the theory of satiation or exhaustion steps in. Perceptual psychologists proceed from the notion that, after a certain period of observation, the tiring of the nerve cells opens up the path for a new interpretation. But it also happens that people who have not been told there is a second meaning never construct one, no matter how long they may look at the drawing.

Again, experiments have shown that there are ways of influencing hich image is seen first. Test subjects who were told in advance that they would see an old woman saw her first. Showing them a photo of an old woman beforehand was also enough to guide their perception.

Once we know that there is more than one meaning, naturally the situation becomes quite different. Then we are able to guide our own perception ourselves, and switch at will between the different meanings. And so another theory suggests that what we see depends more on memory associations than on the 'tiredness' factor.

In *The Upside-Downs*, a comic strip that ran in the *New York Herald* from 1903 until 1905, another form of ambiguity was used. With this, perception was reorganized by turning the picture upside down. There are many such pictures which offer a new meaning by way of a 180° turn. What was special about Gustave Verbeek's work, however, was the fact that one could invert the whole strip, which consisted of six pictures, and read two totally different stories.

Knowledge of figure and ground can also save lives. Camouflage is simply the ability to flout as many rules as possible concerning the division between figure and ground. The more difficult it is to separate the two, the greater the chances of avoiding or at least delaying being seen. In the animal kingdom especially, this is a considerable advantage when it comes to survival.

Many fish, for example, have darker backs and lighter bellies, so that from above they are difficult to see against the dark depths, whereas from below they are harder to distinguish against the bright surface of the water. Fish that live near the bottom also have a pattern which is difficult to discern against the sea bed, even from close up.

Other fish look like seaweed, and cuttlefish can change their colour to that of the place where they happen to be. This is also the special talent of the most famous quick-change artist on land, the chameleon, which with a little bit of luck you will find illustrated bottom right.

Zebras' stripes do not, of course, help to hide them in the steppes, but they are herd animals, and so when they crowd together, it is difficult for predators to distinguish between figure and ground, and thus to see where one animal ends and the other begins.

Camouflage is also an important military device. Camouflage nets can make vehicles and camps invisible from the air, and camouflage uniforms provide good protection for soldiers. There are different colours and patterns to fit in with the various types of landscape. For forested areas, we have the well-known combination of green and brown, but in the desert the clothes will be sand-coloured, and in snow, of course, they are white.

From left to right: *My Wife and My Mother-in-Law, My Husband and my Father-in-Law,* and *Family Portrait,* with an old man, an old woman and a young woman

Panel from Gustave Verbeek's comic strip *The Upside-Downs*, 1903

Images from a German edition of *Asterix and the Big Fight*. The Roman legionaries have not quite grasped the art of camouflage.

Camouflage in nature and on the battlefield can save lives.

CAN WE BELIEVE OUR EYES? OR DO THEY LIE TO US?

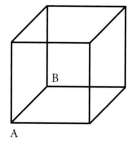

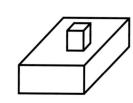

Left, the Necker cube. If you look at the tops of the cube and box on the right-hand side, the cube will appear to be inside the box. If you look at the bottoms, it will seem to be on top.

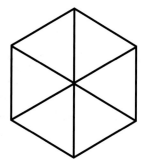

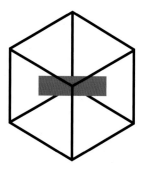

We see the Kopfermann cube as a two-dimensional drawing, unless we are given extra information, like the bar in the variation below.

We can only see in two dimensions. But it's hard to believe that statement. How is it, then, that we can estimate distances, drive cars, play tennis, or deliberately pick things up? If we had a three-dimensional retina, there would be nothing special about our being able to see in three dimensions. Where images are represented on the retina, we would have a reliable and complete set of data about distances. The retina, however, only provides us with a flat, two-dimensional image. The third dimension of depth that we perceive is just a construction created by our visual system.

We know that a drawing can only be a two-dimensional surface. We can test this by simply touching the page. And yet we do not see Bridget Riley's painting opposite as something flat. On the contrary, we see waves. And no matter how hard we try, it is impossible for us to view this painting as being two-dimensional. Logically, then we should come to the conclusion that one of our senses is delivering false information. But because experience teaches us otherwise, in this case we shall have to trust our hand rather than our eyes.

This apparent defect in our visual system, however, is in fact the basis of our ability to perceive depth. In order to explain this, we must take a look at the basic features of depth vision.

The raw material delivered by the retina allows an infinite variety of interpretations of spatial depth. When just one of this vast range is selected – and is agreed on by everyone else in a general consensus – then clearly the construction of depth must follow certain rules. Donald D. Hoffman calls these the 'rules of universal vision'. They must be extremely efficient, since they reduce the number of interpretations from a huge number to just one or two.

The Necker cube – named after its inventor, the physicist Louis Albert Necker – is also a two-dimensional picture, and yet we can 'see' a cube. What is more, our perception can shift, and at one moment we can see A as the front, and the next moment B. Which variation we see, and for how long, seems to be beyond our control.

Have you ever asked yourself the following questions: when we're

Mario Balloco: Blobs of
colour are recognized
immediately as three-
dimensional objects by
means of shadows.

Bruno Ernst creates the
illusion of depth with
chessmen and colour.

The pictures on the right
and left are the same,
turned upside down.

not looking, is A at the front or B?
Or neither? How can it happen
that two people look at the same
cube at the same moment, and one
sees A at the front, and one sees B?
As we construct the cube and have
different possible ways of doing so,
there can be no clear – and above
all, no right or wrong – answers to
these questions.

The fact is, however, that the
figure forces us to construct a
cube in accordance with particular
rules, even though we could also
see it as a two-dimensional line
drawing. We do the same with the
Kopfermann cube on page 226.
This drawing initially seems to us
to be flat, though it could also
represent a cube. Why, then, in
this instance do we decide against
spatial depth?

According to Hoffmann, the most
important rule is to construct only
those visual worlds for which the
picture offers a lasting view.

This simple rule explains many
optical illusions, including the
Kopfermann cube. In addition to
the cube, there are countless
possible interpretations. For
example, a tetrahedron seen from
below, a prism with subdivisions,
a hexagon split into triangles. But
with all these constructions, the

interpretation would be the chance
product of one specific viewpoint.
The image of a cube would
therefore imprint itself on the
retina only from one such
viewpoint, and a tiny movement to
the left or the right would result
in a different image. The three-
dimensional construct would in
this case be a very unstable
interpretation, and consequently
we opt for a two-dimensional one.

For centuries, philosophers,
scholars and scientists were
unable to agree on whether depth
perception was inborn or learned
by experience from a very early
age. Even now, there can be no
definitive answer, because it
involves a combination of
different mechanisms, behavioural
patterns and thought processes.
The complexity of all these
becomes clear if we briefly survey
the most significant findings of
research in all these fields.

To begin with, we can divide visual
perception into two categories:
monocular vision (with one eye)
and binocular (with both). The
latter is dependent on the position
of the eyes in relation to one
another, and the manner in which
the eye muscles function.

One crucial binocular factor is
disparity. This results from the
distance between the eyes –
around six centimetres. Within
this span, each eye sees an object
or scene from a different angle.
3-D films and images exploit the
difference by using technical
means to show slightly staggered
images to the left eye and the right
eye. This is also the principle on
which 3-D glasses are based.

Another factor is convergence.
Here, the axes of sight meet at the

object on which they are trained, and the pupils come closer together as the object comes closer (ultimately making us go cross-eyed). The fact that this is a muscular operation becomes evident if we move a finger centrally towards our eyes. The tightening of the muscles, and their relaxation as the object moves further away, is evaluated by the brain as an indicator of distance. However, the angle is only significantly different over very short distances, and so this means of evaluation is comparatively vague and limited to things in close proximity.

Accommodation is the term used to describe the fact that our lenses must focus on the object, just like a camera. This again is a muscular action. The tension of the muscle varies according to the distance of the object, and so this too provides us with information about distance. But once again, the mechanism is only reliable when the object is within a range of about two metres.

We all know about motion parallax from our experience of sitting in a moving train or car. If we look out of the window, objects seem to move past at different speeds. Those that are closer move faster, and those that are further away move more slowly.

The monocular factors are those that allow spatial vision even with one eye. They are also called image factors, because we are used to deriving them from such things as photographs, paintings, drawings and other two-dimensional representations. They include perspective, overlap, with one object situated behind another, and the known size of things.

Shadows also give an indication of depth.

The extent to which shadows influence our perception of depth can be gauged from the photographs of the European space mission 'Mars Express', reproduced at the bottom of the opposite page. They show landscapes that no human had ever seen before. The one on the right is exactly the same as the one on the left, but the other way up. Our perception constructs two totally different landscapes, even though the information is identical. You can test this for yourself by turning the book upside down.

The reason for this is simple: we start from the fact that light always comes from above. On the basis of this premise, we interpret the patches of light and the shadows to decide what constitutes highs and lows.

In the Chiesa del Gesù, where does the wall end and the ceiling begin?

Shigeo Fukuda shows us an impossible staircase.

The man on this ladder in Paris is only a painting.

Before the discovery of central perspective, artists had to make do with temporary solutions, like the column.

The length and breadth of these two tables are identical.

The cube keeps shifting between convex and concave.

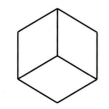

The Schröder staircase, with a variation

M.C. Escher's *Convex and Concave*. The left half is painted convex, and the right half concave.

The conveyance of depth through overlap was the most common method used in painting right through to the Renaissance in order to depict objects in a spatial context. When there were difficulties of perspective, painters had to resort to temporary solutions, as in the example shown top left. In this picture, there is no vanishing point, and so in order to conceal his problem, the artist placed a column at the point where the floor tiles should have met. Many paintings from this time have an alienating effect on us, because we sense that the proportions are not right and everything seems too flat.

In 1410, a milestone in art history took place with the discovery of central perspective by the sculptor and architect Filippo Brunelleschi.

Despite our recognition of central perspective as being a correct element in our way of seeing things, it is not an essential, let alone a unique precondition for our perception of depth. Mathematical and geometrical drawings often use parallel perspective. In this, all the lines of an object that run parallel to one another are drawn parallel, as in the Necker cube and the Schröder steps. There is no vanishing point. This does not correspond to our customary vision or to what is imprinted on our retina, but we still have no difficulty deciphering what we see. Nevertheless, this kind of perspective does involve some phenomena that show just how fragile our system of spatial organization really is.

One of the most striking examples of how easily we can be manipulated is the drawing of two tables, above left. Even if I tell you that their dimensions are precisely the same, you will still happily bet a tidy sum on their being different. And even after you have measured them, and confirmed that they are indeed the same, you will still find it impossible to change your original view. The left-hand table remains narrower and longer than the one on the right. I'm afraid no one has yet found an explanation for this particular optical illusion.

Below is another cube puzzle. Unlike the Necker cube, in which we saw the external and internal lines simultaneously, this cube shifts between concave and convex. At one moment we see the outside, and the next we see the inside of the cube.

The same principle is to be seen in the Schröder steps. At first sight, the dots appear to be on one step. Note that we tend to separate the steps according to their convex edges. After a while, though (or if we turn the book upside down), our perception reverses itself, and convex edges become concave. Then we divide the steps up in a new formation, and see that the dots are now on different ones.

M. C. Escher used this mechanism to create the striking image *Concave and Convex*. Thanks to its ingenious construction, we see the left half as convex and the right as concave. If you find this difficult, first cover one half and then with your eyes, follow one of the men on a ladder into the picture. As soon as you cross the middle, the picture will irresistibly reverse itself, and what was previously the floor will now become the ceiling.

We can only have blind trust in the rules of construction that govern our three-dimensional perception, for they provide the basis for our orientation in the third dimension. And the fact that we do this so unconditionally is what allows artists to play optical tricks on us, with all their impossible objects.

The best known of these is undoubtedly the impossible triangle. In this, we have a conflict between vision and logic. Even though it is clear to us that such a construction is not logical, we cannot distinguish a single point which is visually 'wrong'. There is no solution to this clash between eyes and reason – we can see the triangle quite clearly, even though we know that we should not be able to see it. If that sounds confusing, it is no more so than the confusion inflicted on our sense of vision, and in the end we can only give up, because we shall never be able to find fault with the drawing.

The impossible three-beam construction has fascinated so many people that countless models and drawings have been made out of all kinds of materials. It can even be built in three dimensions, although it will only look like the drawing when seen from one precise viewpoint.

That is also the explanation for the impossible triangle. We trust so completely in the rule that we would construct something impossible, even though we know that it cannot be right, rather than violate that rule. And the rule is the same one that explained the Kopfermann cube. The impossible triangle can exist, as many photos have proved, but only from one precise viewpoint. With just the slightest movement to left or right, it breaks up and the deception is exposed.

What we see here is precisely what our visual intelligence excludes as a possibility when it transforms two-dimensional into three-dimensional representations. In real life, the chances of our getting such a spot-on view are next to none.

The illustration on the right may help to make this clearer. Here we see a spatially stable and logical-looking construction. But put your finger over the point at which the ends of the bars overlap, and once again you are confronted with the impossible triangle.

Similar mechanisms are at work with the impossible steps. And even these can be built in 3-D. But the moment you move away from the designated standpoint, the construction has little resemblance to the painting or drawing, as can be seen from Shigeo Fukuda's model of Escher's *Waterfall*, below right.

In conclusion, it can be said that we construct spatial depth out of the two-dimensional images received by the retina. This is why we are so susceptible to well-constructed deceptions.

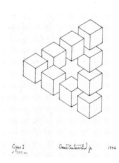

Left: One of the first impossible objects, painted by Pieter Breughel; Right: Oscar Reutersvärd's impossible triangle

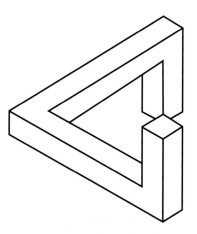

If you put your finger or a pencil over the open ends, this drawing, which is perspectively correct, becomes an impossible triangle.

Above: M. C. Escher's *Ascending and Descending*, and Andrew Lipson and Daniel Shiu's Lego version; Below: M. C. Escher's *Waterfall*, and Shigeo Fukuda with his own model version

THE VISUAL BRIDGING OF DISTANCE

Burt Lancaster in Paris, 1955

Chuck Norris and Bruce Lee in the film *Way of the Dragon*, 1973

We only believe what we see with our own eyes. On the other hand, you can't necessarily believe what you see. Especially in the realms of film and photography, the weaknesses of our perception of depth are often shamelessly exploited. We always see a three-dimensional scene reduced to a flat-surfaced medium, and as depth is something we have to construct for ourselves, it is easy to deceive us.

The fact that distances can only be determined by a process of construction has already been demonstrated earlier. Exactly how we set about this process is naturally of great interest to those who earn a fortune – or hope to save a fortune – by means of optical illusions. It is therefore hardly surprising that in the film industry, where costs can soar into the tens of millions, trickery is used whenever possible.

Although we know that neither actors nor stuntmen get hurt in a fight, we see every kick and every punch as if it landed. The face or body of the person receiving the blow ensures that we can't tell whether it actually landed or

missed by a foot. The fight is so well rehearsed and choreographed that the illusion is perfect.

What is crucial, however, is that the camera should be positioned at exactly the right angle. Just as we have seen with the impossible, three-dimensional objects, the wrong angle will immediately betray the deception and destroy the illusion.

Many magic tricks, like those of the sword-swallower, would be impossible without this weakness in our vision.

It is evident that we humans love to play around with such effects. Near the Eiffel Tower in Paris there is a famous spot where every day hundreds of tourists take the same photo. You can position yourself in such a way that on the photo it looks as if you have the tower in the palm of your hand or growing out of your head.

There are just as many photos of people seemingly pushing the Leaning Tower of Pisa in an effort to straighten it out – which of course is all good for the tourist trade.

If we do not make
a clear distinction
between foreground
and background...

...we end up with
unusual scenes.

William Hogarth,
False Perspective, 1754

In such photos, we are fully aware of the optical illusion. All the same, it appears that we cannot resist the urge to establish a connection between objects that in fact are spatially far apart from one another.

In the photo on page 233, we see the famous illustrator Saul Steinberg, who in 1952 was visiting the photographer Lee Miller in England. Together they went to see the Long Man of Wilmington, a 70-metre-high, prehistoric chalk drawing of a man. When they were about half a mile away, they had the idea of taking a photo with Steinberg's hand seemingly drawing the man.

The two photos at the top of this page give us a slight visual shock. At first we can't decide whether we should really believe the sight we think we see. However, as we are pretty sure that there is no such thing as a four-armed man or a two-headed camel, we very quickly uncover the deception. All the same, every time we look at it, we still tend to see the impossible.

The painter and engraver William Hogarth devoted one particular work to the problem of depicting foreground and background in a two-dimensional medium. He wanted to show all the things that could go wrong, and so he gave the picture the following subtitle: 'Whoever makes a Design without the Knowledge of Perspective will be liable to such Absurdities as are shown in this Frontispiece.'

For example, the wayfarer (top right) is lighting his pipe with the candle of the person leaning out of the top-floor window. The whole scene is riddled with similar perspective blunders. With this

picture, Hogarth unwittingly paved the way for all the impossible objects. What the moralist intended as a warning and a deterrent to his colleagues actually made him godfather to the ads reproduced in Chapter 3, *Foreground and Background*.

It seems that we get so much pleasure from these anomalies that we are quite happy to overlook the fact that they are based on a defect in our visual system.

Have a good look at
this ship before you
turn the page.

ARE TEN METRES A LOT OR A LITTLE?

Horizontal-vertical illusion: A-B looks shorter than C-D, but is in fact longer.

Surprised?

If you ask someone a question like that, the answer will always be: 'For what?' For a car it's a lot, for a plane it's a little.

'How big is big, and how small is small? And how big must something be for it no longer to be small?' asked Til Schweiger in the film *Der Eisbär*. If you have no additional information, you can't possibly answer.

We need a reference in order to evaluate size, as we can see from the example of the ship on the left. A well-made model can't be distinguished from the original unless we have a point of comparison.

This fact can save you a lot of money if you're making a film. Even though nowadays a great deal of the post-production work is done by computer, you will find scarcely any films that don't use models somewhere. This is particularly the case with explosions, sci-fi effects and famous buildings if permission has been refused to film there. The models are so perfect that we cannot possibly know that we are being tricked.

Luckily, there is a phenomenon known as 'size constancy' which ensures that we don't have to doubt everything we see.

An object that is far away from us will convey a much smaller image to the retina. In spite of this, a face which is half a metre away will not seem a great deal smaller to us than when the person is standing three metres away, although in fact the size of the image on the retina has been reduced to a sixth. If you look at your hand in front of your eyes, and then stretch it out at arm's length, you won't have the impression that it changes size.

We always incorporate perspective and surroundings into our perception. That is why a cinema screen looks enormous, even if we're sitting in the back row. From the sofa in the living-room, the TV set may occupy a larger proportion of our field of vision, but it still seems a lot smaller.

Size constancy functions less well in the vertical. Even from an insignificant height, things seem a lot smaller than they do from the same horizontal distance. Anyone

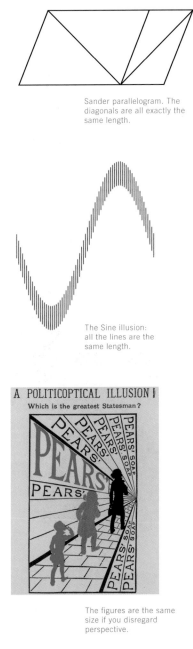

Sander parallelogram. The diagonals are all exactly the same length.

The Sine illusion: all the lines are the same length.

A POLITICOPTICAL ILLUSION
Which is the greatest Statesman?
PEARS'

The figures are the same size if you disregard perspective.

The couple next to the front left column are the same size as the couple at the far end of the colonnade.

who stands on a diving board in a swimming pool will confirm this impression.

Sculptors sometimes compensate for this defect by distorting the perspective of their statues at the top. A rider will be proportionately bigger than the horse, and his head will be bigger than his feet.

This principle was already known to the Ancient Greeks. Many columns were built with a gradually increasing circumference towards the top. This balances out the perspective distortion, so that the columns look dead straight from below.

Neither sculptors nor the ancient Greeks, however, thought of making such corrections on the horizontal plane. We are quite used to the effect there, and so any correction would seem in itself to be a distortion.

That can be seen very clearly in the Pears' Soap illustration on the left. Here we are deceived because the size constant has deliberately been ignored. The three figures on the poster are all exactly the same size. The fact that we do not see them that way is scarcely surprising, because according to perspective they ought to be progressively smaller the further back they are in space. Then we would judge them to be the same size, even though in absolute terms they would be different.

The same phenomenon is to be seen in the picture bottom left. The tiny couple by the left-hand column are exactly the same size as those in the background. You can measure this for yourself. Nevertheless, we have the

impression that those at the back are 'normal' size, whereas those at the front seem the size of mice.

An extremely impressive example is the drawing top right on the opposite page. This is a spatial variant of the Müller-Lyer illusion (a line with an arrowhead pointing inwards seems shorter than the same length line with an arrowhead pointing outwards). You will already have guessed that the two dark lines are exactly the same length.

Because of the perspective layout of this scene, and although we are now fully aware of the truth, we still refuse to perceive these lines as being even approximately the same. Our perception simply doesn't work that way. Or at least not until we hide everything except the lines themselves. To set your mind at rest, measure them yourself.

The mechanism of size constancy is not, incidentally, confined to humans. Most animals have it as well. Indeed this ability is crucial for their survival, as they must be able to recognize and work out the size of a potential enemy from a distance, and not wait till it is standing right in front of them.

We can see from a three-dimensional example that illusions can be created in reality as well as on paper. A favourite experiment in science museums is the room named after Adelbert Ames, who invented it in 1946. Many variations have been constructed since then. From outside the room, you look with one eye through a peephole situated at a particular point. From here it appears to be rectangular, with its doors, windows, ceiling and floor.

In actual fact, though, it is a trapezium in which everything has been so arranged and painted that from just this one precise viewpoint it seems rectangular.

It is our experience that makes us 100 per cent certain that rooms are rectangular, and have floors and ceilings at right angles, and so we cling to that perception even if the facts are against us.

If two people enter the room and each stand in a corner, we will see one as being much smaller than the other. If they change places, and go from one corner to the other, we might even decide that one has grown and the other shrunk, rather than question the nature of the room. In actual fact, the person in the one corner is almost twice as far away and goes uphill into the corner nearer to the observer.

Here too, the background to this is the size constant. We always see people in their perspective position relative to ourselves. As we have formed the opinion that the room is as we see it, we can't place the person in the correct spatial relation to ourselves. Our perspective correction mechanism is thrown right out of gear.

Differentiating between large and small always entails relating things to one another. If there is no reference point, we cannot form any judgment about size.

The fish in the picture on the bottom right is probably not familiar enough for you to recognize it and know what its 'normal' size should be. You can only gauge its size if you can compare it with other objects that you know.

If you cover the hand in the top left corner, the fish looks like the catch of the century, because you take the fisherman as your comparative reference. But if you cover the angler and uncover the hand, you can scarcely imagine the fish providing a meal even for two.

Our visual dependence on our surroundings is also evident from objects which we see every day, either at home or outside. If we move house, for instance, we may well be surprised at how small our large sofa seems when it's standing in the street. Or the surfboard that never seemed particularly large down at the beach suddenly becomes enormous when we're looking for cupboard space to store it for the winter.

A spatial variant of the Müller-Lyer illusion: the dark lines are the same length.

Ames Room: the men are all about the same height.

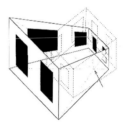

Sketch of an Ames Room

Cover the fisherman, and then cover the hand.

THE WHOLE IS GREATER THAN THE SUM OF ITS PARTS

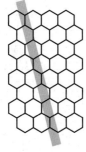

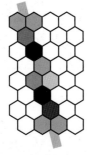

A hexagonal representation of the retina and the patterning of a line

When the form is right, we are more flexible with regard to the content. We possess a remarkable talent for abstraction when it comes to recognizing shapes, whereas much of what you saw in Chapter 5, *Compositions*, would remain invisible to most animals as well as from the most expensive computers. They will never grasp more than part of the meaning, and so you should be proud that you can see what you can see!

In 1918, a 21-year-old photographer named Arthur S. Mole got 21,000 soldiers and officers to stand in formation and create a portrait of the then president, Woodrow Wilson. Astonishingly, we have no difficulty at all in seeing the face of the president, as opposed to the figures of the individual soldiers. In fact, it is virtually impossible for us *not* to see the portrait.

This kind of representation has now become familiar to us at special events. For instance, on major sporting occasions we often see people in the stadium raise coloured boards at a given signal, to form flags, team logos or sponsorsip messages.

The fact that we find it so easy and indeed such fun to put different elements together and create a new whole is perhaps due to the nature of our perception. In order to understand this, we must retrace our steps and consider exactly how our retina is constructed.

On page 209 we read that there are rods and cones on the retina, and these cells are laid out next to one another: the cones are mainly in the area of the fovea centralis, where our vision is at its most acute, while the rods are more towards the outer areas.

Let us assume that we are gazing at a black line. The information on the retina will look something like the drawings on the left. In the areas where the line meets a large section of the cell, the nerve cell reacts strongly; where the line only grazes the nerve cell, the response is weaker.

Out of these different reactions from the countless individual cells, we reconstruct the image of a sharply defined line. Human vision, then, is always an act of arranging and assembling many individual pieces of information.

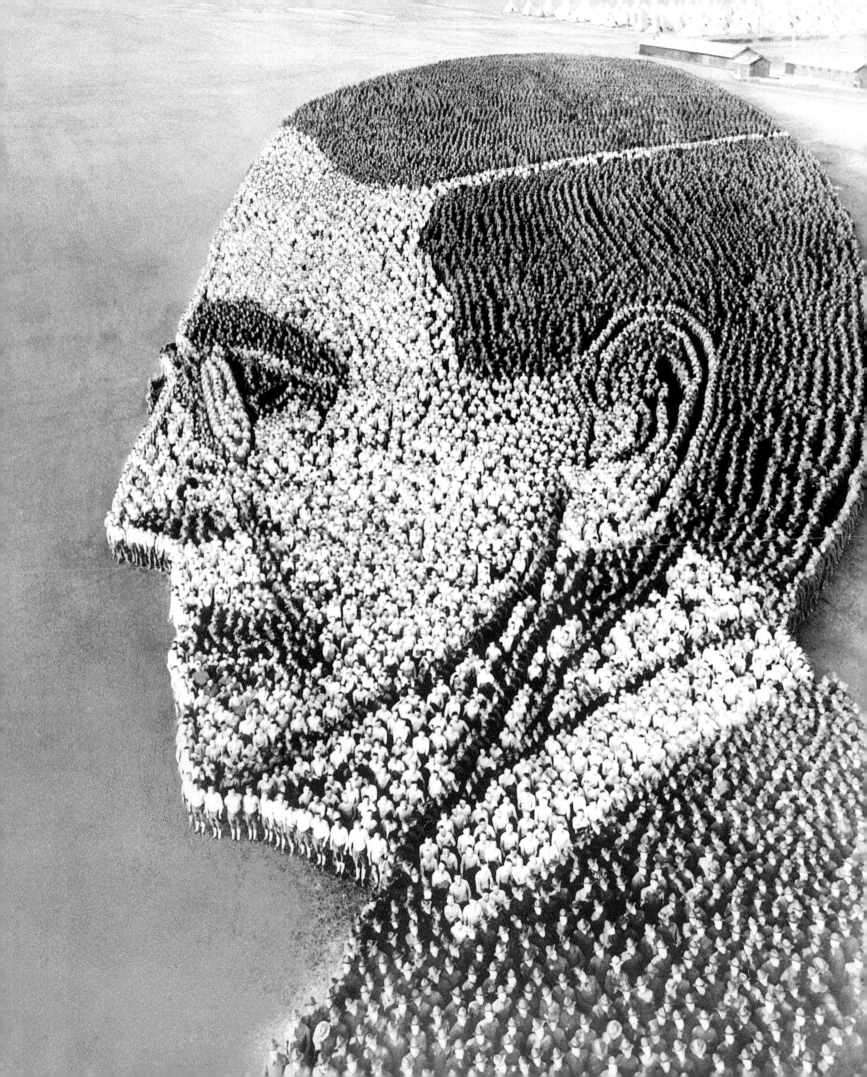

The compound eyes of a fly

A deer hunt mosaic from Pella, 375–300 BC

Detail and complete picture: Vincent van Gogh, *The Garden of St Paul's Hospital*, 1889

In stark contrast to the faceted images familiar to us from horror movies, insects with so-called compound eyes see things in much the same way as we do. Through their many individual eyes, their vision assembles the bits and pieces just as our nerve cells do on the retina. The only difference is that our patterns are far more detailed and refined than those of the insects.

Another important factor is that we are accustomed to working with such patterns. Most printing processes involve a grid of varying complexity. When we look closely at a large-format poster, we can see this quite clearly, and many neon signs are constructed with a dot matrix grid.

One of the oldest known figurative mosaics dates from 375–300 BC: the hunting scenes from the Macedonian Greek city of Pella. Evidently the pleasure of using small components to create a new and larger whole is nothing new.

This, in fact, is the basic principle of painting. After all, a cooperative observer looking at a picture will see much more than a piece of canvas containing brushstrokes and patches of colour. If you stand back from the picture, the subject will impose itself all the more forcibly on your attention, so that you will see a landscape, a still life, a portrait or a battle scene.

However, if you are in a gallery and stand so close to a large painting that the attendant starts getting nervous, you will focus mainly on the individual strokes and the artist's technique, and you will have difficulty seeing the content at all.

The fact that the whole is greater than the sum of its parts is the central tenet of Gestalt theory, or Gestalt psychology. This approach to our understanding of perception became popular at the beginning of the 20th century. When we perceive something as a whole, it is never an isolated unit but is always the product of different factors. Gestalt theory seeks to determine these factors, together with the principles that guide us when we organize and assemble the individual components.

This is not just a matter of our being able to decipher the patterns in the different forms we observe; we are also able to extrapolate formations from multiple objects, as we can see from the example of the skulls in the pictures at the top of this page.

Here we are following a principle that might be called 'visual stability of form'. As soon as the outline makes us recognize an overall meaning which is different from that of the individual components, we perceive it just as clearly – if not more clearly – than the latter.

It is this capacity for perception beyond the object itself that distinguishes us from many animals, which would not be able to recognize such formations. The same capacity is also the cause of many a headache for experts who are trying to build the faculty of sight into computers.

This kind of pattern recognition can only work on things that are familiar to us. They must already have been stored in our memory. That is why we have no difficulty at all in recognizing all the signs below as 'A' or 'a', even though they are very different. But someone who had no knowledge of the alphabet would not see an 'A' in these shapes, and he might well insist that most of them had nothing in common. Likewise, someone who had never seen a skull would look at the pictures on the right and see only what is actually depicted there – an arrangement of female figures in the first one, and a woman in front of a mirror in the second.

Even when we have two or more pictures, we look for connections that will extend beyond the individual images. We are eager to construct additional meanings that are not to be found in the pictures themselves. Thus an observer will have no doubt that the two pictures on the right depict the same giraffe, who is even peeping out of his frame at the top.

 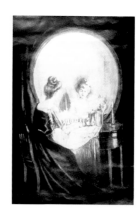

The theme of Vanitas by Dali (left) and Charles Allen Gilbert (right)

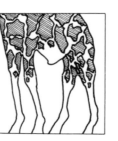

We immediately establish a connection even beyond the scope of a single picture if it seems logical to do so.

HUMANS ARE CREATURES OF HABIT

If you can't recognize this, turn it 90° in a clockwise direction.

We know that the earth does not have a top or a bottom. All the same, we are conditioned always to see maps with the north at the 'top'.

We love it when we can go on using and re-using patterns we have learned. And we quickly allow ourselves to be conditioned by familiar allusions. Our joy at recognizing something we have already learned appears to be so great that we are not even bothered if at second glance we see certain inconsistencies. The aim of a good ad campaign is to exploit this willingness to be conditioned. If we only need one stimulus to make us think of a brand or product, the marketing department has done a good job.

The extent to which we are subject to visual pressures can best be illustrated by showing how easily we can be fooled. Although it is true that some perceptual factors are inborn, the majority are certainly the result of patterns that we have learned. If we are to find our way in the world, it is of vital importance that these patterns should repeat themselves. This is what the artist Michael Schuster exploits in the picture on the opposite page. In various parts of a public building, he installed traffic mirrors, but instead of a reflection, one actually sees a photograph of the reflection.

The effect is startling. We are amazed when we do not see ourselves in the mirror, and we start to doubt our own perception. Then we realize that we have let ourselves be deceived by the typical form of the mirror.

With the maps on the left, we find it to hard to recognize something we have often seen in the past. The reason is that they have been turned 90º and 180º respectively.

These examples also illustrate another important aspect of perception. The process can be subdivided into two stages that follow one another: recognition and identification. First we have to recognize the object – i.e. organize it correctly, separate figure and ground, and establish the correct orientation. Only then does it assume a familiar structure, and we can begin to identify it. To do so, we search our data bank of stored forms and objects in order to find something that corresponds to the image we have constructed. The two processes follow on so quickly from one another that we do not even realize that they are actually different.

AT SECOND GLANCE

Cover of the book *Gesichter* (*Faces*) by François and Jean Robert, with photographs of 130 everyday objects

Two pictures from a series of photos by Alain Giraud: (left) *Grace Jones* and (right) *Cyrano de Bergerac*

We rarely perceive objects in isolation. We see them in contexts that may be dependent on subject, space or associations.

At first sight, we see them exactly as they present themselves to us. Through additional information, we then receive indications that they may have another meaning. At second glance, we reassess the situation and see something we hadn't noticed before.

This additional information generally comes to us through a text or a sender who has set something familiar in a new context. Once we have acquired the extra knowledge, our second viewing leads to a kind of 'aha!' response. Without this knowledge, most people would never cotton onto the new meaning.

A wonderful example is the picture on the opposite page. We see a massage roller. Nothing else. But if you have read this book attentively, another association will occur to you. The photo is also a symbol used by a car manufacturer. If you simply add two words and the company logo, you will get the image of an advertising campaign.

If it still doesn't ring a bell, turn back to page 125.

For twenty years, the brothers François and Jean Robert have been seeking out everyday objects that will turn into faces on a second viewing. The images in themselves will probably not look like faces at first sight, but in the Roberts' book we are looking for everything that might fit under the heading of 'faces', and so suddenly we ourselves can also see people, animals, joy and sorrow.

We may assume that these photographers are now roaming the world with a completely new focus, unable to stop themselves from seeking anything but potential faces.

The photographer Alain Giraud is pursuing a similar dream, photographing ships in dry dock. The titles of his pictures establish sudden and unexpected associations with famous people.

CAN YOU SEE MORE THAN THREE TWIGS ON A SHELF?

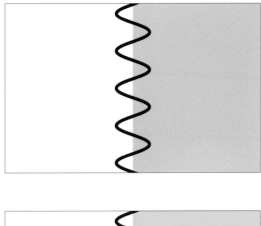

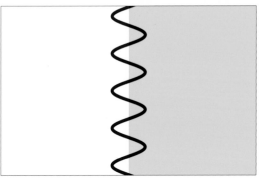

The 'filling-in' phenomenon

Can you make out anything meaningful in these blobs? If not, just turn the page.

Amazing! We can see things that actually aren't there. On the preceding pages we have already learned what masters of construction we are. We create three dimensions, even though we only see two, we have no problem bridging the gap between foreground and background, we assemble individual components into new forms, and we establish contexts that only exist in our mind's eye.

What now follows is even more incredible: we can see objects that do not exist. If you can see more than three branches on the opposite page, then you have once again fallen victim to your passion for construction.

When we look around, our eyes tend to fix especially on outlines. The outline is the border between foreground and background, between object and space. The function of the outline is to point to the area that it encloses.

The phenomenon of 'filling in' is a special feature of the human process of perception. Through different degrees of brightness, the brain looks for these contours, which are always part of the object they enclose.

Place yourself three metres away from this book and then look at the two illustrations on the left. In the top picture, because of the different degrees of grey, our perception will only register variations in brightness. We therefore construct two outlines: one borders the squiggly line as an object in itself, and the other borders the grey area as a second object that lies behind the line.

Something completely different happens with the second picture. The yellow area will be interpreted as an object in full colour, as opposed to a contrast in brightness. The squiggly line will become the outline of this yellow object, and our visual intelligence will even complete the colour by inserting it into the curves that now form part of the object. But the curves that point away from the object will be seen as completely white.

Surprisingly, this effect cannot be seen in the first picture, even though we are the same distance away from it. This is not because

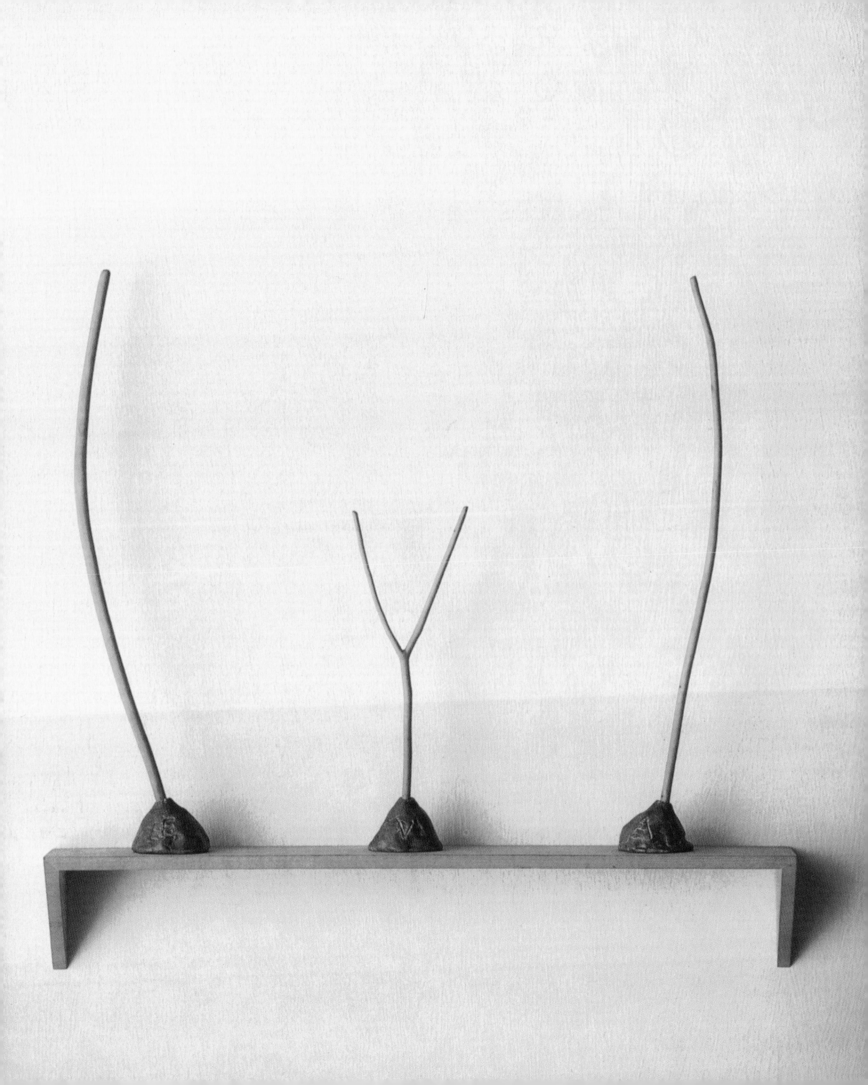

Can you manage to group these dots together without forming any circles?

We see the outlines and the bodies of the two men even though they are not there.

These black lines may look like nothing much, but try turning the book 90° and you'll see what they are.

Kanisza triangle and square. We can see the outlines quite clearly, and the figures seem brighter than the background.

Although you can no longer see the grey blobs as they were on the previous page, you can now clearly make out five Bs.

our vision is imprecise, but because our brain constructs the scene through analysis and interpretation.

Another example of how we complete scenes is the illustration at the bottom of page 248. At first we can make nothing of the grey blobs. So long as we continue to hunt around, we can find no starting point from which we might assemble the individual components into a coherent, familiar form. At the bottom of this page you can see the same grey blobs.

The difference lies in the apparently random pattern of black blobs that has been placed on top of the original collection. Suddenly we have no trouble at all filling in the missing pieces, and can see five Bs underneath – even though the grey blobs are precisely the same as they were on page 248. We need this 'filling in' ability all the time in our daily lives, because objects are seldom to be seen full size and completely out in the open. It can be of crucial importance for us to identify them clearly by constructing these missing elements.

A small example of our passion for finding outlines can be seen in the dotted pattern at the top of this page. It is almost impossible not to construct little circles out of the dots – even if one does so only momentarily.

This creative gift for constructing and filling in outlines is as fascinating for artists and graphic designers as it is for scientists. They too know that we enjoy it, and that our attention is heightened when we can complete things for ourselves.

The art of omission stimulates our imaginations – and we love it. It doesn't matter it's part of a picture, a novel, a play, a film or anything else – if everything is laid out on a plate for us, we tend to get bored quite swiftly. It's no coincidence that the maxim 'less is more' can be found in most of the world's languages.

An example of illusory outlines is to be seen in the picture of two men on the left. We can see both of them in full evening dress, even though the artist has only drawn a few individual features. The hands, for instance, are in no way linked to the body.

In the picture below that, all we can see at first is a jumble of black shapes that don't seem to have any meaning. If you need help, just turn the book 90° clockwise, and you will immediately see the German word 'Hilfe', which means help!

These are what we call 'subjective letters'. The technique is commonly used to make the letters stand out more by means of shading. What is fascinating about it is that the shading is limited to one side, and yet the letters seem complete to us. We think we can perceive the outlines.

Illusory outlines entail a double deception. On the one hand, we construct an outline that doesn't exist; on the other, we think we can see a different degree of brightness between the illusory figure and the background.

The increase in brightness is very clear in the subjective figures of the Kanisza triangle and square in the next drawing, which functions in accordance with the same principle. The notches in the circles make us construct a triangle or square with clear outlines that appear to be much brighter than the background.

There is no measuring apparatus in the world that can confirm what you think you see. The white of the paper is, logically, equally bright everywhere. And yet we can't stop ourselves from seeing the figures that appear to be imposed on the circles. We even assume that the circles themselves are complete and are underneath the white figures. But if we slowly cover these black circles, the equally clear figures will also disappear.

It is also possible not to see a figure, or at least to take some time finding it – as in the drawing top right. In this apparently random collection of notched circles, we may only discover the subjective triangle after searching for it.

There are variations on this illusion in the other illustrations. In the first, we can see the letters VP straight away, and the picture below makes it evident that we can also construct subjective circles.

The Ehrenstein illusion is derived from a variation on the Hermann grid. The broken lines are enough to inveigle us into constructing little circles. We perceive these as being twice as bright as the grid around them.

There is a special feature near the bottom left-hand corner of this grid. Here two circles intersect, and the tendency is for us to see them as a rectangle. Experiments have actually shown that if we are relaxed, we tend to perceive

subjective circular shapes, but once we start to concentrate, we substitute squares for circles. Try it for yourself.

As for why we construct these subjective outlines, once again there is no definitive explanation. All the different theories have their weak points, and there is not one so far that cannot be contradicted in some way.

The phenomenon is far from new. Even in cave paintings from 30,000 to 10,000 BC, our ancestors were working with subjective outlines.

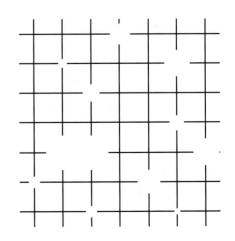

Here it takes us a little longer to construct the subjective triangle.

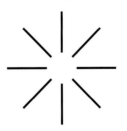

Letters can also be constructed in the same way.

Circles can be constructed too.

While looking through a physics book in 1870, the Berlin physiologist Prof. Ludimar Hermann stumbled across this page, and thus by accident discovered one of the most famous illusions. You can't stop yourself from seeing the grey dots at the intersecting points of the white lines.

Ehrenstein illusion

LINGUISTIC PICTURES AND PICTORIAL LANGUAGE

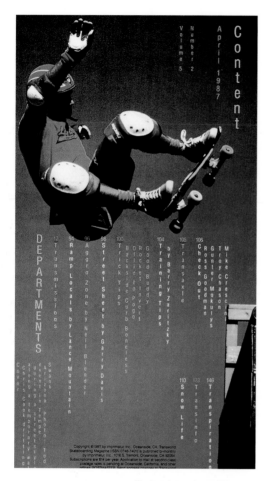

We do not perceive words as individual letters but as pictures. If the writing runs vertically instead of horizontally, our system of recognition cannot function, and we realize what an effort it is to read words letter by letter.

The Italian designer Italo Lupi found this alphabet on the beach.

Any technique that uses a system of fixed signs and symbols in order to convey information through a medium is defined as linguistic. Interestingly, the visual process works in exactly the same way as any other pictorial stimuli.

Pictographs were the ancestors of all forms of writing. For a long time, it was assumed that the Sumerians had invented writing, and that other cultures imported the idea. Today, though, it is believed that there were similar, independent developments in different cultures. This is borne out by new finds in Southeast Europe (5300 BC), Egypt (3320 BC), China (2000 BC), and the remains of the Maya culture in Central America (*c.* 1200 BC).

Every writing system began with pictographic representations of objects or beings. Subsequently, these signs were linked together in order to establish meaningful contexts — what we call ideograms.

Over the centuries, the signs began more and more to represent the sounds of spoken words rather than the object itself. This was the beginning of phonetic script.

During this phase of transition, in order to differentiate between a pictograph and a phonogram, more signs were developed — the so-called determiners.

Even though our words consist of individual letters, their form is very important for the way we read: bcesaue it dsoen't mettar what squecene the leterts of a wrod are in, so long as the frist and lsat leterts are in the rhigt pitosoin. We read words as a whole. It only becomes difficult when texts are exclusively in lower or upper case, or the letters run downwards instead of across, as in the illustration top left. Then our pattern-seeking faculties cannot latch on.

Incidentally, not all forms of writing have been deciphered. One of the best-known unsolved mysteries is the Phaistos Disc from Crete, on the opposite page.

THE OLDEST HARD-DISK EVER	Description by Jean-Jacques Mouris, Luxembourg.				
Manufacturer	Unknown	Capacity	Double-sided, low density	Data Security	Readable for over 3,000 years
	Made in Crete		Tracks/face: 5 (single spiral)	Safety	Fire- and earthquake-resistant
Date manufactured	2nd half 17th century BC		239 symbols total (43 different) in 61 files		Water-resistant after fixing-process
	to 2nd half 16th century BC		face A: 120/31 (symbols/files)	Original location	Minoan Palace of Phaistos (Crete/Greece),
Type	Read-Write (RW) (before fixing process)		face B: 119/3		storage archive with fire-resistant walls
	Read-Only (RO) (after fixing process)		file separators: vertical bars	Current location	Archeological museum, Iraklion (Crete/Greece)
System	Write: Physical engraving	Character Type	Protolinear	Availability	No longer in production;
	Read: Optical	Speed	(R,W) variable (software control);		one unit still in stock
Size	Diameter: 6 inches (16 cm)		up to 5 rpm (reading) on outermost tracks	Contents	No reliable software for file decryption
	Thickness: 5/8 inch (16 mm)	Power requirements	Heat-source for fixing-process		currently available

LIE ON YOUR BACK AND READ THE CLOUDS

A fully automated reading of coffee grounds is even available on the Internet. A rose indicates a happy future with much joy and good health.

The original Rorschach tests are naturally not available for publication. This is a picture from Andy Warhol's *Rorschach* series, 1984.

Even if this sounds nice and relaxing, it really gets our sense of sight working. In nature we can always find a multitude of materials, objects and surfaces that will satisfy our desire to construct meaningful patterns.

Reading the clouds is a game, and it's also fun. We can go wild and impose the craziest identities on those blobs of vapour in the sky. There is a similar process at work when fortune-tellers read tea leaves. This practice may go back to the Middle Eastern tradition of reading coffee grounds: both processes involve pouring the dregs of the drink into a saucer and then trying to make out symbols and figures in the resulting shapes.

Such attempts to look into the future may well be greeted with a scornful smile by most people, but psychologists too make use of our desire to find a meaning in the most arbitrary of visions.

The Rorschach test was published in 1921 by the Swiss psychologist Hermann Rorschach. It works as follows: the people being tested are presented with ten standard cards containing ink blots. They are asked to say what they can see in these random patterns. A trained psychologist then compares their answers to those of a control group. The aim is to gather information about people's intelligence and state of mind without having to ask direct questions.

The test is widely used and helps in making decisions, for instance about whether convicts should be allowed out of jail, candidates for the priesthood should be ordained, pilots can fly, and alleged victims of abuse are telling the truth. It is, however, controversial and is never used as the sole criterion. This is partly because there are now a lot of advisers who may give away the answers that are most favourable to the candidate's cause.

COLOUR COMES FROM THE BRAIN

CocaCola-Red
McDonalds-Yellow
Dairy Milk-Purple
COLOUR
Doublemint-Green
Nivea-Blue
Tango-Orange

We have internalized some colours to such a degree that we can see them straight away in our mind's eye.

Colour swatches help to maintain colour constancy in the printing process.

blue	yellow	red	green	yellow	blue
green	red	yellow	blue	red	green
yellow	yellow	green	red	yellow	yellow
red	green	red	yellow	green	red
yellow	red	blue	green	red	yellow
green	blue	blue	red	blue	green

These words for colours do not match up with the colours that they are printed in.

Sir Isaac Newton was the pioneer of research into colour perception. By 1704 he had developed a colour spectrum which is still valid today. Through his experiments with prisms, he discovered that visible light contained all colours.

If we study the whole spectrum of light waves, we will see that humans can only perceive a small proportion of them, and our whole world of colour is confined to this tiny section. Many animals, on the other hand, can perceive wavelengths within the ultraviolet and infrared zones. Exactly what they see, and whether they perceive our colour zone differently from us, we cannot tell.

The manner in which colour comes into being is explained by physics. Colourless light meets, for example, a tomato, which absorbs the blue, green and yellow components and only reflects the red. These same components also meet the retina in the eye, and we see the tomato as red – provided, of course, that it is ripe.

All our perceptions of colour are are dependent on the wavelength of the reflected light. These waves stimulate certain nerve cells on the retina, and these impulses in turn stimulate reactions in the brain. So now you know that it's not a question of red, blue and green, but of physical processes.

It needs to be stressed, though, that there is no intrinsic colour in the wavelength either. The one that creates a sense of redness in us is just as invisible as those of the other colours. Even though you can actually measure this wavelength, the 357 nanometres will no more trigger off a colour construct than RAL-Code 3001 without the corresponding colour sample.

Colour sensitivity is therefore a very subjective thing, because colour is also something we construct. You can see evidence of this on the opposite page. If we can bear to look at the MacKay illusion for more than a second without feeling dizzy, we will see colours in a drawing which is quite clearly composed only of black lines on a white background.

Like so much else, this phenomenon still awaits a satisfactory explanation. It is

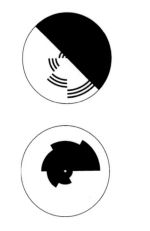

Benham's top: when it rotates, we see colours.

Alfons Schilling with his painted and spinning discs

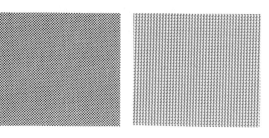

From a certain distance, we see both surfaces in the same shade of grey.

probably caused by the fact that we never make an absolute decision about colours, but always relate them to colours in surrounding areas. If we come really close to the centre of the illustration, our whole visual apparatus is overwhelmed, and so we make 'mistakes'. Bees would not see these colours, because they can perceive and distinguish the nuances much more efficiently than we can.

These 'shimmering' colours also provide the basis for the spinning top invented by the games designer C. E. Bentham in 1894, which is still sold all over the world. When the top starts to rotate, we see red, green, blue and violet rings. More than 100 years later, scientists still don't know why.

Alfons Schilling has turned the idea of the top into an art form, by painting rotating discs. In his exhibitions, they are mounted on a motor and at specified intervals they start spinning, thereby changing colour.

The same phenomenon can, however, be reversed, and we can turn colours into grey. You can see from the illustrations at the bottom of the page that at a certain distance from the observer, the grids turn the same shade of grey.

Even two surfaces of exactly the same colour can have a completely different colour effect. This is because we always incorporate our surroundings in the process of colour construction. A particularly significant role is that of subjectively perceived brightness. An almost incredible example of this is the illustration at the top of the opposite page. You will only

believe that the two greys are identical when you cover the rest of the picture.

Another example, this time in colour, is Jan Koenderink's two squares below. Here we can see just how much influence light has on our perception of colour. In the square on the left, we not only see individual areas of colour, but we also perceive sources of light that appear to illuminate the scene. In the respective corners, we see a yellow, red, blue and green light. In the right-hand square, we see no additional light sources but just a surface that is evenly illuminated by a 'white' light.

This is because we interpret gradual changes of colour, in terms of strength and brightness, as being due to a different light, whereas sudden changes are seen as the result of new surfaces – i.e. new colours or objects. That is why we interpret the colours of the two squares differently, even though their colours are identical.

Is our sense of colour perception defective? The answer is both yes and no. Yes, because we are not measuring instruments, and we do not perceive colours as absolute values. No, because all this is underpinned by a system. It is called colour constancy, and it adapts itself to different lighting conditions.

Light can have very different colours. Sunlight in the morning is quite different from sunlight in the evening. Halogen lamps are a different colour from neon lights. Sunglasses can be green, orange, brown or blue, and yet once we have got used to them, our view of the world through these tinted lenses results in our seeing more or less the same colours as when we are not wearing them.

We call this ability to adapt 'approximate colour constancy'. It is called approximate because the colours do in fact change a little. When we've been on holiday for a few days, we are delighted to switch on the light above the mirror and admire our tan. But in the neon light of a changing room, it can no longer be seen. The light that's used in the fruit and vegetable section of your local supermarket is a very 'sunny' one, so that everything looks fresher and juicier.

A similar trick has been used in the picture bottom right. Thanks to the pattern of red lines on the packaging, the carrots themselves look redder than they really are. When you unwrap them at home, prepare to be disappointed.

The difference lighting can make to colours is evident when you go past a block of flats at night. The windows are all different colours. And yet each occupant in each room will still see a white sheet of paper as white.

It is interesting that on the one hand we can perceive the finest nuances of colours, but on the other, because of the effects of colour constancy, we find it very difficult to pin down or describe colours clearly. You can test this by looking at the illustration that graduates from red to orange. If we cover one of the dividing lines with a pencil, the colours of the two areas seem to blend. It is as if our visual system carries out a colour correction, so that we can believe that the two colour surfaces are in fact one.

Colour must also be viewed as a product of culture. The ancient Greeks had no word for blue, and even in the Middle Ages there was no English word for orange. We can perceive something like 20 million shades of colour, and yet we have only about 7,500 terms for them. That is one reason why it is so difficult to describe colours.

In every language there are words for black and white. If there is a third word, then it is always for red. If there is a term for a fourth colour, it is either green or yellow. The fifth, of course, is whichever of these is not the fourth. The next in line are blue and then brown. If there are eight or more, they are purple, pink, orange and grey, in no particular order.

The claim that the Eskimos have hundreds of words for the different types of snow has proved to be famously false. Nevertheless, they do have seven different terms for white. It is certainly true that the environment has a major influence on definitions of colour. Peoples living in the African desert, for example, have no word for green but they have five for red. The French use two words for brown ('brun' and 'marron'), whereas the Chinese, Japanese, Welsh and Inuits don't have a single one.

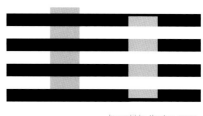

Incredibly, the two greys are the same.

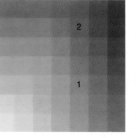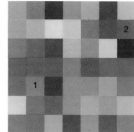

In both squares, the sections with the same numbers are the same colour.

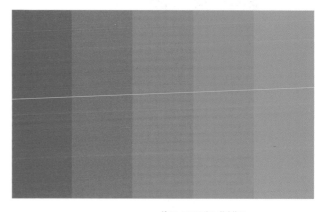

If we cover the dividing lines with a pencil, the adjacent sections seem to be the same colour.

Because of the red pattern on the packet, the carrots look a lot fresher.

This index with its
impressive list of agencies
is also a huge thank
you. My deepest respect,
admiration and gratitude
goes to all those whose
creativity has made this
book possible. With their

#12 INDEX

infectious love of design,
they prove over and over
again that the greatest of
all creative fears – that
everything has been
done before – is patently
without foundation.

INDEX OF AGENCIES

#1

Wirz Werbung AG
Uetlibergstraße 132
CH-8045 Zurich
Switzerland
Tel. +41 44 45 75 757
www.wirz-werbung.ch

McCann-Erickson, Paris
48 rue de Villiers
92300 Levallois-Perret Cedex
France
Tel. +33 14 14 91 402
www.mccann.com

Wirz Werbung AG
Uetlibergstraße 132
CH-8045 Zurich
Switzerland
Tel. +41 44 45 75 757
www.wirz-werbung.ch

GGK Zürich Werbeagentur AG
Bruno Züttel
Seefeldstraße 229
CH-8043 Zurich, Switzerland
Tel. +41 44 38 86 969
www.ggk.ch

Publicis Mojo Australia
2000 Sydney
Australia
Tel. +61 29 25 89 000
www.publicismojo.com.au

Springer & Jacoby Werbung
Poststraße 14-16
20354 Hamburg
Germany
Tel. +49 40 35 60 30
www.sj.com

Scholz & Friends Berlin
Wöhlertstraße 12/13
10115 Berlin
Germany
Tel. +49 30 28 53 53 00
www.sfberlin.de

Prof. Uwe Loesch
Mettmanner Straße 25
40699 Erkrath
Germany
Tel. +49 21 15 58 48
www.uweloesch.de

Scholz & Friends, Berlin
Chausseestraße 8/E
10115 Berlin
Germany
Tel. +49 30 59 00 530
www.sfberlin.de/berlin/uk

GPP. Werbeagentur GmbH
Heilbronner Str. 154
70191 Stuttgart
Germany
Tel. +49 71 12 55 07 300
www.gpp.de

Springer & Jacoby Werbung
Poststraße 14-16
20354 Hamburg
Germany
Tel. +49 40 35 60 30
www.sj.com

Ogilvy & Mather, Frankfurt
Darmstädter Landstraße 112
60598 Frankfurt am Main
Germany
Tel. +49 69 96 22 50
www.ogilvy.de

VVL/BBDO
Scheldenstraat 122
1080 Brussels
Belgium
Tel. +32 24 21 22 00
www.vvl.bbdo.be

Duval Guillaume, Bruessel
Antwerpselaan 40
1000 Brussels
Belgium
Tel. +32 24 12 08 88
www.duvalguillaume.com

#3

Niklaus Troxler Graphic Design
Bahnhofstraße 22
6130 Willisau
Switzerland
Tel. +41 41 97 02 731
www.troxlerart.ch

Bates / Red Cell, Oslo
Hoffsveien 1E
0213 Oslo
Norway
Tel. +47 22 87 97 00
www.bates.no

Scandinavian Design Group
Sandakerveien 24 C
0402 Oslo
Norway
Tel. +47 22 54 95 00
www.sdg.no

Euro RSCG Worldwide, France
Allée de Longchamp 2
92281 Suresnes Cedex
France
Tel. +33 15 84 79 000
www.eurorscg.com

Wolfgang Scheppe
mail@wolfgangscheppe.com

Pierre Mendell Design Studio
Widenmayerstraße 12
80538 Munich
Germany
Tel. +49 89 21 99
www.mendell-design.de

Springer & Jacoby Werbung
Poststraße 14-16
20354 Hamburg
Germany
Tel. +49 40 35 60 30
www.sj.com

Ambience D'Arcy Advertising
Neelam Centre 401-e, A-Wing
400025 Mumbai
India
Tel. +91 22 24 96 28 98 305
www.ambiencedarcy.com

Young & Rubicam, São Paulo
Rua General Furtado do
Nascimento 9, CEP 05465-
070 São Paulo, Brazil
Tel. +55 11 30 26 44 00
www.yrbrasil.com.br

Niklaus Troxler Graphic Design
Bahnhofstraße 22
6130 Willisau
Switzerland
Tel. +41 41 97 02 731
wwww.troxlerart.ch

Ogilvy & Mather
Darmstädter Landstraße 112
60598 Frankfurt am Main
Germany
Tel. +49 69 96 22 50
www.ogilvy.de

Cheil Communications America
3351 Michelson Drive Suite 390
Irvine, CA 92612
USA
Tel. +1 949 975 7380
www.ccaworld.com

Trikaya Grey Advertising
Mumbai
400 013 Mumbai
India
Tel. +91 224 93 93 36
www.grey.com

Shigeo Fukuda
1-9, 2-703 Chuo, Kuki-shi
Saitama Prefecture
Japan

Theme Media & Production
70 Bendemeer Road
#02-02
Singapore 339940
Tel. +65 68 41 43 11

Saatchi & Saatchi, London
80 Charlotte Street
London W1A 1AQ
United Kingdom
Tel. +44 20 7636 5060
www.saatchi.co.uk

VS Propaganda
Rua J. Carlos 101
22461-130 Jardim Botanico
Rio de Janeiro, Brazil
Tel.+55 21 25 27 58 23
www.vspropaganda.com.br

Campbell Doyle Dye
4 Utopia Village, Chalcot
Road, London NW1 8LH
United Kingdom
Tel. +44 20 7483 9800
www.cddlondon.com

Ogilvy & Mather Santiago
Avenida dell Parque 4161
Huechuraba, Santiago
Chile
Tel. +56 26 70 39 00
www.ogilvy.com

JWT London
1 Knightsbridge Green
London SW1X 7NW
United Kingdom
Tel. +44 20 7656 7000
www.jwt.com

Leo Burnett, Singapore
33 Pekin
#03-01 Far East Square
Singapore 048763
Tel. +65 62 36 17 77
www.leoburnett.com

Euro RSCG Ball, Singapore
82 Telok Ayer Street
#02-01 Far East Square
Singapore 048467
Tel. +65 63 17 66 00
www.eurorscg.com

Bayerische Immobilien Gruppe
Thomas Empt
Communications Design
Tel. +89 92 387 11
E-Mail: th.empt@bayerische-
immobilien.de

DDB, Paris
Rue d'Amsterdam 55
75391 Paris Cedex 08
France
Tel. +33 01 53 32 56 69
www.ddbparis.fr

Neogama/BBH
04552-050 São Paulo
Brazil
Tel. +55 11 33 65 12 55
www.neogamabbh.com.br

#2

Springer & Jacoby Werbung
Poststraße 14-16
20354 Hamburg
Germany
Tel. +49 40 35 60 30
www.sj.com

CLM / BBDO
Allée des Moulineaux 2
92441 Issy-les-Moulineaux
France
Tel. +33 14 12 34 123
www.bbdo.com

JWT Hamburg
Elbberg 1
22767 Hamburg
Germany
Tel. +49 40 30 61 90
www.jwt.de

#4

Dentsu, Tokyo
1-8-1 Higashi-shimbashi
Minato-ku, 105-7001 Tokyo
Japan
Tel. +81 36 21 65 111
www.dentsu.co.jp

Carmichael Lynch
800 Hennepin Avenue
Minneapolis, MN 55403
USA
Tel. +1 612 334 6000
www.carmichaellynch.com

Florian Bachofen,
Nicole Domokos,
Andrea Dübendorfer
Photographer:
www.alfonsosmith.com

Scholz & Friends Berlin
Wöhlertstraße 12/13
10115 Berlin
Germany
Tel. +49 30 28 53 53 00
www.sfberlin.de

Saatchi & Saatchi, Madrid
Plaza Santa Ana 7
28012 Madrid
Spain
Tel. +34 91 15 12 000
www.saatchi.com

Czajkowski & Brajdic
00-790 Warsaw
Poland

BMP DDB London
12 Bishops Bridge Road
London W2 6AA
United Kingdom
Tel. +44 20 7258 3979
www.ddblondon.com

Colenso BBDO
College Hill 100, Ponsonby
Auckland 1002
New Zealand
Tel. +64 93 60 37 77
www.colensobbdo.co.nz

Leo Burnett USA
35 West Wacker Drive
Chicago, IL 60601
USA
Tel. +1 312 220 5959
www.leoburnett.com

Saatchi & Saatchi
Kongens Nytorv 18
1050 Copenhagen
Denmark
Tel. +45 33 93 79 80
www.saatchi.com

Colenso BBDO
100 College Hill, Ponsonby
Auckland 1002
New Zealand
Tel. +64 93 60 37 77
www.colensobbdo.co.nz

CLM / BBDO
Allée des Moulineaux 2
92441 Issy-les-Moulineaux
France
Tel. +33 14 12 34 123
www.bbdo.com

Hill Holliday Boston
200 Clarendon Street
Boston, MA 02116
USA
Tel. +1 617 437 1600
www.hhcc.com

DDB Red, Madrid
Lopez de Moyos 145
28002 Madrid
Spain
Tel. +34 91 45 64 400
www.ddb.es

Stenstrom Advertising
Nybrokajen 7
11186 Stockholm
Sweden
Tel. +46 85 62 85 000
www.stenstrom.se

BATEY / Red Cell
12 Jalan Wan Kadir 1
60000 Kuala Lumpur
Malaysia
Tel. +60 32 27 72 72 299
www.bateyredcell.com.my

H.Stern
Rua Garcia D'Ávila, 113
Ipanema, Rio de Janeiro
Brazil
Tel. +55 21 21 06 00 00
www.hstern.com.br

BBH, London
60 Kingly Street
London W1B 5DS
United Kingdom
Tel. +44 20 7734 1677
www.bbh.co.uk

DevarrieuxVillaret, Paris
164, Rue de Rivoli
75001 Paris
France
Tel. +33 15 32 92 929
www.devarrieuxvillaret.fr

Tiempo BBDO, Barcelona
Tuset 5
08006 Barcelona
Spain
Tel. +34 93 30 69 000
www.tiempobbdo.com

#5

Exclam Agencia
Rua Tapajos 542
80510-330 São Francisco,
Curitiba, Brazil
Tel. +41 24 08 000
www.exclam.com.br

Bates Brasil
04571-010 Sao Paulo
Brazil
Tel. +55 11 55 03 74 55
www.newcommbates.com.br

Leo Burnett, Singapore
33 Pekin
#03-01 Far East Square
Singapore 048763
Tel. +65 62 36 17 77
www.leoburnett.com

Publicis Frankfurt GmbH
Walther-von-Cronberg-Platz 6
60594 Frankfurt am Main
Germany
Tel. +49 69 15 40 21
www.publicis-frankfurt.de

DDB Bern
Felsenaustraße 17
3000 Berne
Switzerland
Tel. +41 31 30 04 242
www.ddb.ch

The Jupiter Drawing Room
The Terraces, Fir Road
Observatory, Cape Town
South Africa
Tel. +27 11 23 38 968
www.jupiter.co.za

McCann-Erickson BCA
Voltastraße 31
60486 Frankfurt am Main
Germany
Tel. +49 69 79 40 40
www.mccann.de

TBWA \ Paris
Rue de Billancourt 162-164
92103 Boulogne-Billancourt
Cedex, France
Tel. +33 14 90 97 010
www.tbwa-france.com

Sullivan Higdon & Sink
255 N. Mead
Wichita, KS 67202
USA
Tel. +1 316 263 0124
www.wehatesheep.com

Hill Holliday Boston
200 Clarendon Street
Boston, MA 02116
USA
Tel. +1 617 437 1600
www.hhcc.com

Weber, Hodel, Schmid, Zurich
Switzerland
Agency no longer exists.

Contemporanea
Praia do Flamengo, 200
6° andar Cep 22210-030
Rio de Janeiro, Brasil
Tel. +55 21 25 55 66 85
www.contemporanea.com.br

kwp! Melbourne
18 Stokes Street
VIC 3207 Port Melbourne
Australia
Tel. +61 39 64 79 500
www.kwp.com.au

Stenstrom Advertising
Nybrokajen 7
11186 Stockholm
Sweden
Tel. +46 85 62 85 000
www.stenstrom.se

BBDO Singapore Pte Ltd
8 Shenton Way
#38-01 Temasek Tower
Singapore 068811
Tel. +65 65 33 22 00
www.bbdo.com

Leo Burnett, Warszawa
Ul. Karmelicka 9
00-155 Warsaw
Poland
Tel. +48 22 86 09 800
www.leoburnett.com

Ambience Publicis, Mumbai
Neelam Centre 401-E, S.K.
Ahire Marg, Worli
400025 Mumbai, India
Tel. +91 22 24 96 28 98
www.publicis.com

Sullivan Higdon & Sink
255 N. Mead
Wichita, KS 67202
USA
Tel. +1 316 263 0124
www.wehatesheep.com

KNSK Werbeagentur GmbH
Alte Rabenstraße 1
20148 Hamburg
Germany
Tel. +49 40 44 18 901
www.knsk.de

Q Werbeagentur
Nymphenburger Str. 125
80636 Munich
Germany
Tel. +49 89 55 299 101
www.q.ag

JWT Barcelona
Via Augusta 281
08017 Barcelona
Spain
Tel. +34 93 41 31 414
www.jwt.es

Jung von Matt/Alster
Glashüttenstraße 38
20357 Hamburg
Germany
Tel. +49 40 43 210
www.jvm.de

Mukai & Associates, Tokyo
Japan

Jung von Matt/Alster
Glashüttenstraße 38
20357 Hamburg
Germany
Tel. +49 40 43 210
www.jvm.de

DDB Berlin
Neue Schönhauser Str. 3-5
10178 Berlin
Germany
Tel. +49 30 24 08 42 34
www.de.ddb.com

Leo Burnett, Portugal
Rua das Flores 7
1200-193 Lisbon
Portugal
Tel. +35 12 13 26 08 00
www.leoburnett.pt

Bates Red Cell, Oslo
Hoffsveyen 1e
N-0213 Oslo
Norway
Tel. +47 22 87 97 00
www.bates.no

BBH London
60 Kingly Street
London W1B 5DS
United Kingdom
Tel. +44 20 7734 1677
www.bbh.co.uk

Jung von Matt / Alster
Glashüttenstraße 38
20357 Hamburg
Germany
Tel. +49 40 43 210
www.jvm.de

Jung von Matt / Alster
Glashüttenstraße 38
20357 Hamburg
Germany
Tel. +49 40 43 210
www.jvm.de

Jung von Matt / Alster
Glashüttenstraße 38
20357 Hamburg
Germany
Tel. +49 40 43 210
www.jvm.de

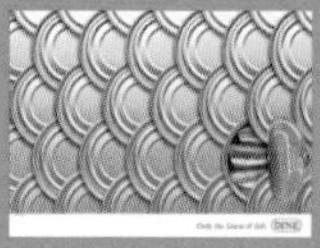

Grey Advertising, Sydney
Level 18, 100 Miller Street,
North Sydney NSW 2060
Australia
Tel. +61 29 93 62 700
www.greyworldwide.com.au

Ubachs Wisbrun
Watertorenplein 4
1051 PA Amsterdam
Netherlands
Tel. +31 20 48 86 888
www.ubachswisbrun.nl

Advico Young & Rubicam
Meisenrain 39
8044 Zürich-Gockhausen
Switzerland
Tel. +41 44 80 19 191
www.ayr.ch

McCann Erickson, Zürich
Rigistraße 9
8033 Zürich
Switzerland
Tel. +41 44 36 84 242
www.mccann.ch

DDB Madrid
Lopez de Moyos 145
28002 Madrid
Spain
Tel. +34 91 45 64 400
www.ddb.com

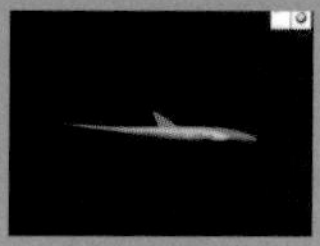

*S,C,P,F..., Madrid
Zurbano 23, 1a
28010 Madrid
Spain
Tel. +91 70 23 434

Schumacher, Jersild
Wessman & Enander
Sergels Torg 12
11487 Stockholm
Sweden
Tel. +46 8 50 61 31 00

Nail Communications
77 Eddy Street
02903 Rhode Island
USA
Tel. +1 401 331 6245
www.nail.cc

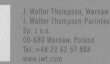

Bates Italia
Via Panama 12
00198 Roma
Italy
Tel. +39 68 44 03 81
www.bates.it

Springer & Jacoby Werbung
Poststraße 14-16
20354 Hamburg
Germany
Tel. +49 40 35 60 30
www.sj.com

Unicer - Bebidas de Portugal
Portugal
Tel. +35 12 29 05 21 00
www.unicer.pt

Young & Rubicam, São Paulo
Rua General Furtado do
Nascimento 9, CEP 05465-
070 São Paulo, Brazil
Tel. +55 11 30 26 44 00
www.yr.com

J. Walter Thompson, Warsaw
J. Walter Thompson-Parintex,
Sp. z o.o.
00-680 Warsaw, Poland
Tel. +48 22 62 57 888
www.jwt.com

Attack CMG
33 Mohamed Sultan Road
238977 Singapore
Singapore
Tel. +65 62 35 01 73

Shigeo Fukuda,
1-9, 2-703 Chuo, Kuki-shi
Saitama Prefecture
Japan

Leo Burnett, Warszawa
Ul. Karmelicka 9
00-155 Warsaw
Poland
Tel. +48 22 86 09 800
www.leoburnett.com

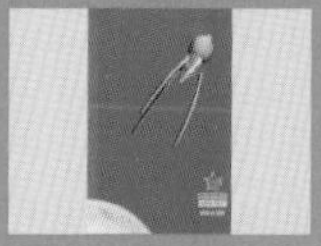

Leo Burnett, Sydney
162 Blues Point Road
McMahons Point
2060 NSW, Australia
Tel. +61 29 92 53 555
www.leoburnett.com.au

MARK / BBDO, Prague
Štulcova 89/4, Nové proboštví
128 00 Prague 2 - Vyšehrad
Czech Republic
Tel. 42 02 21 61 72 01
www.markbbdo.cz

#6

DM9 DDB, São Paulo
Avenida Brigadeiro Luis
Antônio, 5013 Jardin Paulista
São Paulo, Brazil
Tel. +55 11 30 54 99 99
www.dm9ddb.com.br

Lowe Pirella,Milano
20122 Milan
Italy
Tel. +39 02 85 721
www.lowepirella.it

Dentsu Young & Rubicam
Beach Road 300, 30th Floor
The Concourse,
199555 Singapore
Tel. +65 62 95 00 25
www.yr.com

Saatchi & Saatchi, Vienna
Mantlergasse 30-32
1130 Vienna
Austria
Tel. +43 18 78 870
www.saatchi.at

FCB Kobza
Schottenfeldgasse 20
A-1070 Vienna
Austria
Tel. +43 13 79 11
www.fcb.at

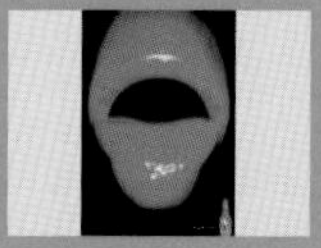

DM9 DDB, São Paulo
Avenida Brigadeiro Luis
Antônio, 5013 Jardin Paulista
São Paulo, Brazil
Tel. +55 11 30 54 99 99
www.dm9ddb.com.br

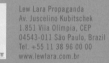

Lew Lara Propaganda
Av. Juscelino Kubitschek
1.851 Vila Olímpia, CEP
04543-011 São Paulo, Brazil
Tel. +55 11 38 96 00 00
www.lewlara.com.br

DDB New Zealand Ltd
80 Greys Avenue
Auckland
New Zealand
Tel. +64 93 03 429
www.ddb.co.nz

Cossette Communication
2100 Drummond Street
Montreal (Quebec) H3G 1X1
Canada
Tel. +1 514 282 4742
www.cossette.com

JWT Company Ltd.
18th Floor, 163 Keelung Road
Section 1
Taipei, Taiwan
Tel. +86 22 74 69 028
www.jwt.com

Ruf Lanz Werbeagentur AG
Eidmattstr. 51
8032 Zürich
Switzerland
Tel. +41 44 38 66 644
www.ruflanz.ch

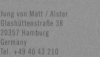

R. Treviño & Asociados
Callejón de los Ayala 101
Despacho 11,Edificio Valle
Real, Col.del Valle,
66268 Nuevo León, Mexico
Tel. +52 83 56 51 78

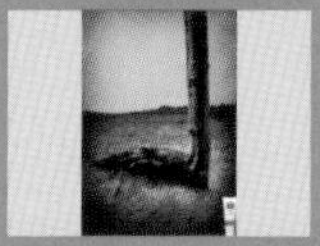

DDB, Hong Kong
Suite 1101, Cityplaza 1
Kings Road 1111 Tai Koo Shing
Hong Kong, China
Tel. +85 22 82 80 328
www.ddb.com

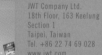

Spillmann/Felser/Leo Burnett
Aemtlerstraße 201
8040 Zürich
Switzerland
Tel. +41 43 31 12 525
www.sflb.ch

Saatchi & Saatchi, Singapore
3D River Valley Road # 03-01
179023 Singapore
Singapore
Tel. +65 63 39 47 33
www.saatchi.com

Jung von Matt / Alster
Glashüttenstraße 38
20357 Hamburg
Germany
Tel. +49 40 43 210
www.jvm.de

GBK, Heye Werbeagentur GmbH
Liprunstraße 16
80335 Munich
Germany
Tel. +49 89 54 24 43 2
www.gbkheye.de

Scholz & Friends, Berlin
Wöhlertstraße 12/13
10115 Berlin
Germany
Tel. +49 30 28 53 53 00
www.sfberlin.de

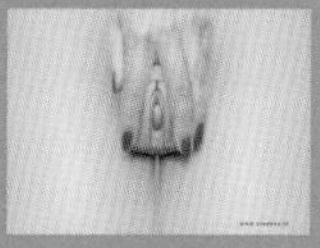

Publicis Amsterdam
Prof. W. L. Kelsomlaan 12
1183 DJ Amstelveen
Netherlands
Tel. +30 20 40 61 200
www.publicis.nl

McCann Erickson, Hamburg
Neuer Wall 43
20354 Hamburg
Germany
Tel. +49 40 36 00 90
www.mccann.de

JWT + Hostettler + Fabrikant
Hardstraße 219
8005 Zürich
Switzerland
Tel. +41 44 27 77 111
www.jwthf.ch

Grey, Warsaw
Ulica Przemyslowa 30-32
00-450 Warsaw
Poland
Tel. +48 22 62 26 79
www.grey.com

BDDP & Fils, Paris
5 bis rue Mahias
92100 Boulogne Billancourt
France
Tel. +33 15 53 83 736
www.bddpetfils.fr

Jung von Matt, Spree
Hasenheide 54
10967 Berlin
Germany
Tel. +49 30 78 95 60
www.jvm.de

Publicis, Madrid
Pº de la Castellana 83 9ª
28046 Madrid
Spain
Tel. +34 91 55 58 411
www.publicis.es

Walker Werbeagentur
Blaufahnenstrasse 14
8001 Zürich
Switzerland
Tel. +41 43 24 40 444
www.walker.ag

D'Adda, Lorenzini, Vigorelli, BBDO
Via Lanzone 4
20123 Milan
Italy
Tel. +39 28 80 07
www.bbdo.com

Dentsu, Tokyo
1-8-1 Higashi-shimbashi
Minato-ku, 105-7001 Tokyo
Japan
Tel. +81 36 21 65 111
www.dentsu.co.jp

Leo Burnett, Hong Kong
6th Floor, Cityplaza 3
14 Taikoo Wan Road
Hong Kong, China
Tel. +85 22 56 74 333
www.leoburnett.com

DDB Madrid
Lopez de Moyos 145
28002 Madrid
Spain
Tel. +34 91 45 64 400
www.ddb.com

Saatchi & Saatchi, Singapore
3D River Valley Road # 03-01
179023 Singapore
Singapore
Tel. +65 63 39 47 33
www.saatchi.com

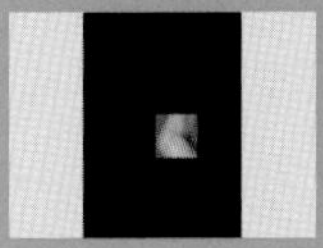

Lowe Ginkgo, Montevideo
Av. Sarmiento 2265
Montevideo
Uruguay
Tel. +598 27 11 61 61
www.loweginkgo.com

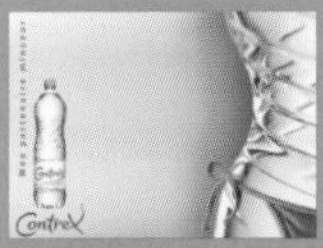

Australie, Paris
Rue Aristide Briand 14
92300 Levallois Perret
France
Tel. +33 14 75 82 200
www.australie.com

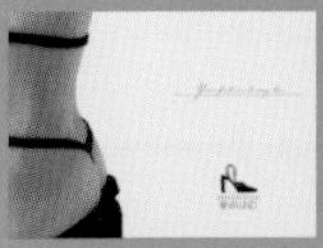

Grey Worldwide Chile, S.A.
5th Floor Las Condes
Isidora Goyene Chea 3365
Santiago, Chile
Tel. +56 23 69 69 00
www.grey.com

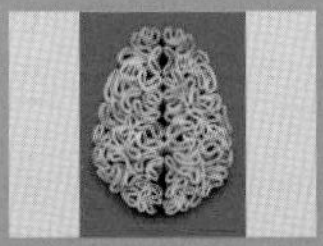

Ogilvy & Mather, Singapore
The Ogilvy Centre
Robinson Road 35
Singapore 068876
Tel. +65 62 13 78 99
www.ogilvy.com

McCann Erickson, Zürich
Rigistraße 9
8033 Zürich
Switzerland
Tel. +43 44 36 84 242
www.mccann.ch

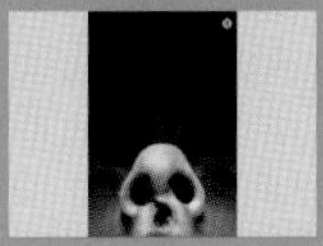

Bassat Ogilvy, Madrid
Enrique Larreta 2
28036 Madrid
Spain
Tel. +34 91 39 84 600
www.bassatogilvy.es

#7

Leo Burnett, Bangkok
3rd floor, Sindhorn Tower 1,
Wireless Road, Patumwan,
10330 Bangkok, Thailand
Tel. +66 26 84 55 55
www.leoburnett.co.th

Springer & Jacoby Werbung
Poststraße 14-16
20354 Hamburg
Germany
Tel. +49 40 35 60 30
www.sj.com

TBWA / Paris
Rue de Billancourt 162-164
92103 Boulogne-Billancourt
Cedex, France
Tel. +33 14 90 97 010
www.tbwa-france.com

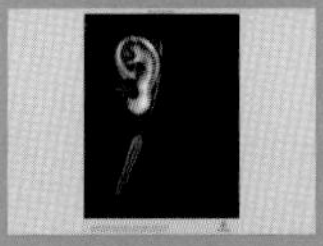

Maher Bird Associates Ltd
82 Charing Cross Road
London WC2H 0BA
United Kingdom
Tel. +44 20 7309 7200
www.mba.co.uk

Jung von Matt / Alster
Glashüttenstraße 38
20357 Hamburg
Germany
Tel. +49 40 43 210
www.jvm.de

Ratto / BBDO, Buenos Aires
Arenales 495
B1638BRC Vicente Lopez
Buenos Aires, Argentina
Tel. +54 11 63 18 22 00
www.bbdo.com

Lowe Lintas GGK, Zürich
Talstraße 80
8001 Zürich
Switzerland
Tel. +41 44 21 59 111
www.loweworldwide.com

Miles Calcraft
Briginshaw Duffy
15 Rathbone Street, London
W1T 1NB, United Kingdom
Tel. +44 20 7073 6900
www.mcbd.co.uk

Dinamo, Lysaker
Fridtjof Nansens vei 16D
1366 Lysaker
Norway
Tel. +47 67 20 00 00
www.dinamo.no

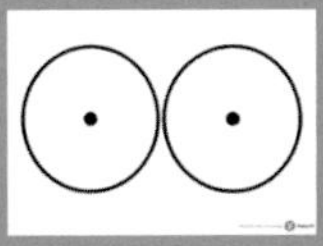

Young & Rubicam, Madrid
Avenido de Burgos 21
Planta 9, Complejo de Torre C
28036 Madrid, Spain
Tel. +34 91 38 42 400
www.yr.com

Wirz Werbung AG
Uetlibergstraße 132
CH-8045 Zürich
Switzerland
Tel. +41 44 457 57 57
www.wirz-werbung.ch

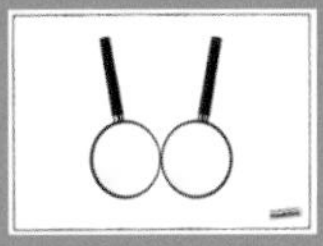

TBWA Hunt Lascaris
49 Wierda Rd West, Sandton,
Johannesburg
South Africa
Tel. +27 11 32 23 100
www.tbwa.co.za

Strusi Estudio Creativo
1060 Caracas
Venezuela
Tel. +58 21 22 65 27 52

Racing Pigeons, Milan
Via Lanzone 4
20123 Milan
Italy
Tel. +39 28 80 07 71
www.racingpigeons.it

DM9 DDB, São Paulo
Avenida Brigaderio Luis
Antônio, 5013 Jardim
Paulista, São Paulo, Brazil
Tel. +55 11 30 54 99 99
www.dm9ddb.com.br

Abbott Mead Vickers
BBDO London
London NW1 5QE
United Kingdom
Tel. +44 20 7616 3500
www.amvbbdo.com

Jung von Matt / Alster
Glashüttenstraße 38
20357 Hamburg
Germany
Tel. +49 40 43 210
www.jvm.de

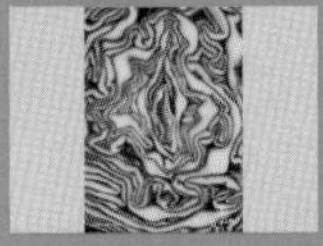

Saatchi & Saatchi, London
80 Charlotte Street
London W1A 1AQ
United Kingdom
Tel. +44 20 7636 5060
www.saatchi.com

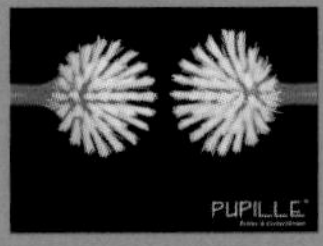

Wüschner und Rohwer
Werbeagentur GmbH
Rosenheimer Str. 143B
81671 Munich
Tel. +49 17 33 77 27 58

Jung von Matt, Offenbach
Ludwigstraße 180d
63067 Offenbach
Germany
Tel. +49 69 82 90 60
www.jvm.de

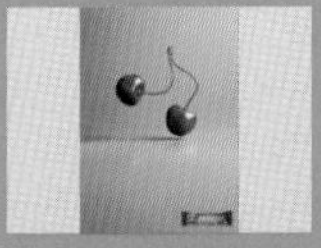

DDB, Vancouver
1600-777 Hornby Street
Vancouver V6Z 2T3
Canada
Tel. +1 604 687 7911
www.ddbcanada.com

McCann Erickson, Wien
Gregor Mendel Straße 50
1191 Vienna
Austria
Tel. +43 13 60 550
www.mccann.at

Leo Burnett, São Paulo
Rua Brejo Alegre 9399
Brooklin, CEP 04557 - 050
São Paulo, Brazil
Tel. +55 11 55 04 13 00
www.leoburnett.com.br

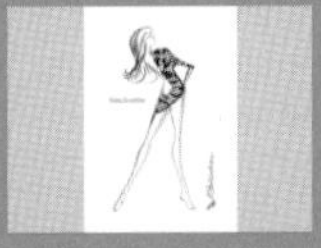

Weigertpirouzwolf
Waterloohain 9
22769 Hamburg
Germany
Tel. +49 40 14 32 390
www.weigertpirouzwolf.de

Yokyor, Amsterdam
Frans van Mierisstraat 92
1071 RZ Amsterdam
Netherlands
Tel. +31 20 57 06 545
www.yokyor.nl

Nazca Saatchi & Saatchi
Paseo de los Laureles 458
Bosques de las Lomas
05120 Mexico City, Mexico
Tel. +52 55 10 84 19 00
www.saatchi.com

Rio Propaganda
Av. Armando Lombardi 205,
Cob 305, Barra di Tijuca
Rio de Janeiro, Brazil
Tel. +55 21 24 93 25 05
www.riopropaganda.com.br

Rafineri, Istanbul
Asmali Mescit Mah. Mesrutiyet
Cad. 233, 34420 Tepebasi
Beyoglu, Istanbul, Turkey
Tel. +90 21 23 34 66 00
www.rafineri.net

Euro RSCG Worldwide
Gutstraße 73
8055 Zürich
Switzerland
Tel. +43 44 46 66 700
www.eurorscg.ch

Saatchi & Saatchi, Singapore
3D River Valley Road #03-01
179023 Singapore
Singapore
Tel. +65 63 39 47 33
www.saatchi.com

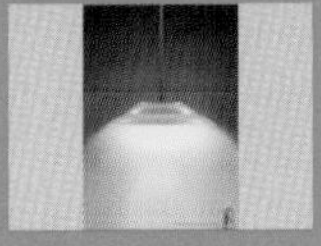

JWT S.p.A.
Via Paolo Lomazzo 19
20154 Milan
Italy
Tel. +39 02 33 63 41
www.jwt.it

DDB Needham, Sydney
Wilcox Mofflin Building
46-52 Mountain Street
Ultimo NSW 2007, Australia
Tel. +61 28 60 28 88
www.ddb.com

Saatchi & Saatchi, Singapore
3D River Valley Road # 03-01
179023 Singapore
Singapore
Tel. +65 63 39 47 33
www.saatchi.com

#8

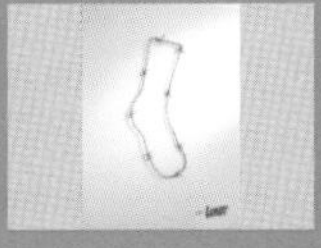

Grey, Warsaw
Ulica Przemyslowa 30-32
00450 Warsaw
Poland
Tel. +48 22 62 26 796
www.grey.com

Dentsu Young & Rubicam
1-11-1 Marunouchi
Chiyoda-ku 100-6209, Tokyo
Japan
Tel. +81 35 21 99 111
www.dyr.co.jp

The Motta Company
9841 Airport Boulevard 600
Los Angeles, CA 90045
USA
Tel. +1 310 348 9955
www.motta.com

Cathedral The Creative Center
Calle Alameda 22
28014 Madrid
Spain
Tel. +34 91 36 90 255

BETC Euro RSCG
Rue du Faubourg Saint-
Martin 85/87
75010 Paris, France
Tel. +33 15 64 13 500
www.betc.eurorscg.fr

Eryk Tam
556112 Singapore
Singapore
Tel. +65 63 82 54 90

Young & Rubicam, Madrid
Avenido de Burgos 21
Planta 9, Complejo de Torre C
28036 Madrid, Spain
Tel. +34 91 38 42 400
www.yr.com

TBWA\LISBOA
Avenida da Liberdade,
38 - 6º, 1250 - 145 Lisbon
Portugal
Tel: +21 32 23 200
www.tbwa.pt

ADK Kyushu
Tenjin 1-chome 9-17
Chuo-ku,810-0001 Fukuoka
Japan
Tel. +81 92 72 14 344
www.adk.jp

BBH, London
60 Kingly Street
London W1B 5DS
United Kingdom
Tel. +44 20 7734 1677
www.bbh.co.uk

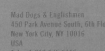

Mad Dogs & Englishmen
450 Park Avenue South, 6th Floor
New York City, NY 10016
USA
Tel. +1 212 675 6116
www.maddogsandenglishmen.com

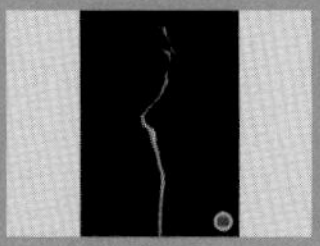

Bates / Saatchi & Saatchi
B. Dmitrovka, 32 Bldg. 4
103031 Moscow
Russia
Tel. +7 09 57 39 09 85
www.saatchi.com

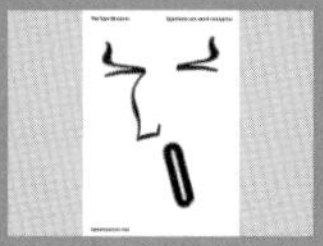

Abbott Mead Vickers BBDO
151 Marylebone Road
London NW1 5QE
United Kingdom
Tel. +44 20 7616 3490
www.amvbbdo.com

Markimage, Lisboa
Rua Marques de Fronteira 8-1°
1070 296 Lisbon
Portugal
Tel. +35 11 38 26 780
www.markimage.com

The Richards Group
8750 N. Central Expressway
Suite 1200, Dallas,
TX 75231-6437, USA
Tel. +1 214 891 5700
www.richards.com

BBCW / Y&R Amsterdam
Adviesbureau voor
Communicatie Karperstraat 10
1075 Amsterdam, Netherlands
Tel. +31 20 57 95 795
www.bbcw.nl

Almap / BBDO, São Paulo
Av. Roque Petroni Jr. 99952
6° e 7° andares
04707-000 São Paulo, Brazil
Tel. +55 11 21 61 56 00
www.almapbbdo.com.br

Leagas Delaney, Hamburg
Waterloohain 5
22769 Hamburg
Germany
Tel. +49 40 54 80 40
www.leagasdelaney.de

Moroch
3625 North Hall Street #1100
Dallas, TX 75219
USA
Tel. +1 214 520 9700
www.moroch.com

McCann-Erickson, Zürich
Rigistraße 9
8033 Zürich
Switzerland
Tel. +41 44 36 84 242
www.mccann.ch

Kolle Rebbe
Werbeagentur GmbH
Dienerreihe 2
20457 Hamburg, Germany
Tel. +49 40 32 54 230
www.kolle-rebbe.de

Jung von Matt / Alster
Glashüttenstraße 38
20357 Hamburg
Germany
Tel. +49 40 43 210
www.jvm.de

Age.Comunicações
12° andar Av. Brigadeiro Faria
Lima, 2055 Jardim Paulistano,
01451-001 São Paulo, Brazil
Tel. +55 11 30 30 03 33
www.age.com.br

DDB Needham, Hong Kong
Suite 1101 Cityplaza One
King's Road 1111, Tai Koo
Shing, Hong Kong, China
Tel. +85 22 82 80 328
www.ddb.com

Seilerzürich
Bühlerstraße
8125 Zollikerberg-Zürich
Switzerland
Tel. +41 44 39 54 100
www.seilerzuerich.ch

Ogilvy & Mather
Darmstädter Landstraße 112
60598 Frankfurt am Main
Germany
Tel. +49 69 96225 0
www.ogilvy.de

Leagas Delaney, Hamburg
Waterloohain 5
22769 Hamburg
Germany
Tel. +49 40 54 80 40
www.leagasdelaney.de

Wunderman Cato Johnson
Beach Road 300, #33 01/03
199555 Singapore
Singapore
Tel. +65 62 95 00 25
www.wunderman.com

Leo Burnett USA
35 West Wacker Drive
Chicago, IL 60601
USA
Tel. +1 312 220 5959
www.leoburnett.com

Sarah Louise Ramsay
9 Edis Street
London NW1 8LG
United Kingdom
Tel. +44 20 7586 1975
www.slrphotography.co.uk

#10

Grey Worldwide Chile, S.A.
5th Floor Las Condes
3365 Isidora Goyene Chea
Santiago, Chile
TEL. +56 23 69 69 00
www.grey.com

TBWA, Paris
Rue de Billancourt 162, 164
92103 Boulogne Billancourt
Cedex, France
Tel. +33 14 90 97 010
www.tbwa-paris.com

TBWA / EPG
Avenida Da Liberdade 38, 6°
1240-145 Lisbon
Portugal
Tel. +35 12 13 22 32 00
www.tbwa.com

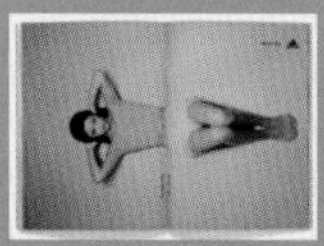

TBWA / Hong Kong
25th Floor, AIA Tower
Electric Road 183, North Point
Hong Kong, China
Tel. +85 22 83 32 033
www.tbwa.com

EMA Price McNabb
1001 Morehead Square Drive
Fifth Floor, Charlotte
NC 28203, USA
Tel. +1 704 375 0123
www.pricemcnabb.com

Grey Worldwide Brazil
Rua Fidêncio Rames 195
6° e 7° Andar CEP 04551-010
São Paulo, Brazil
Tel. +51 11 30 49 82 82
www.greybr.com.br

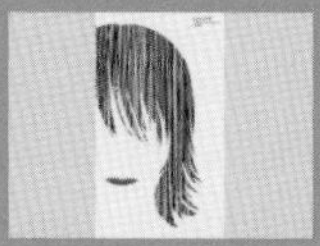

Slingshot
208 N. Market Street, Suite 500
Dallas, TX 75202
USA
Tel. +1 214 634 4411
www.davidandgoliath.com

F/Nazca S&S Publicidade Ltda
Av. República do Líbano 253
04501-000 São Paulo
Brazil
Tel. +55 11 30 59 48 00
www.fnazca.com.br

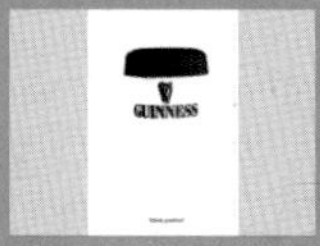

Graffiti BBDO, Bucharest
Turnescu Str. 1A, Sector 5
7000 Bucharest
Romania
Tel. +40 21 22 10 200
www.graffiti.bbdo.ro

Advico Young & Rubicam
Meisenrain 39
CH-8044 Gockhausen
Switzerland
Tel. +41 44 80 19 191
www.ayr.ch

McCann-Erickson S.A.
Paseo de la Castellana 165
28046 Madrid
Spain
Tel. +34 91 56 79 000
www.mccann.com

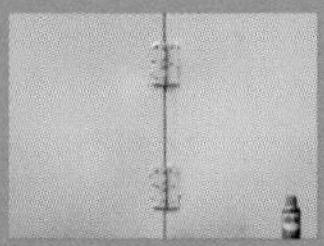

Dentsu Singapore
1 Raffles Place #46-00
048616 Singapore
Singapore
Tel. +65 67 34 01 10
www.dentsu.com.sg

Anderson DDB, Toronto
33 Bloor Street East, 13th Floor
Toronto, Ontario M4W 3H1
Canada
Tel. +1 416 960 3830
www.andersonddb.com

Young & Rubicam
300 Beach Road
199555 Singapore
Singapore
Tel. +65 62 95 00 25
www.yr.com

Weber, Hodel, Schmid, Zürich
Switzerland
Agency no longer exists

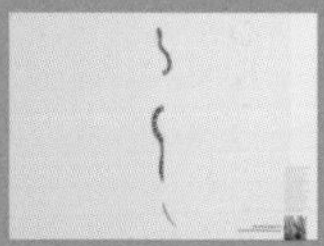

Neogama BBH, São Paulo
Av. Motearrej 174
CEP 05311-000 São Paulo
Brazil
Tel. +55 11 21 84 12 00
www.neogamabbh.com.br

Jung von Matt / Alster
Glashüttenstraße 38
20357 Hamburg
Germany
Tel. +49 40 43 210
www.jvm.de

Aimaq Rapp Stolle, Berlin
Münzstraße 15
10178 Berlin-Mitte
Germany
Tel. +49 30 30 88 710
www.ars-berlin.com

Leo Burnett Publicidade Lda.
Rua das Flores 7
1200-193 Lisbon
Portugal
Tel. +35 12 13 26 08 00
www.leoburnett.com

Scholz & Friends, Berlin
Wöhlertstraße 12/13
10115 Berlin
Germany
Tel. +49 30 28 53 53 00
www.sfberlin.de

Springer & Jacoby Werbung
Poststraße 14-16
20354 Hamburg
Germany
Tel. +49 40 35 60 30
www.sj.com

Publicis, Zürich
Theaterstraße 8
8001 Zurich
Switzerland
Tel. +41 44 26 53 111
www.publicis.ch

TBWA España
4ª Planta, Alfonso XI, 12
Madrid 28014
Spain
Tel. +34 91 53 11 465
www.tbwa.com

McCann-Erickson, São Paulo
Rua Loefgreen 2527
04040-033 São Paulo
Brazil
Tel. +55 11 57 63 000
www.mccann.com

#9

McCann Erickson, Seoul
7th Floor Maehun Building
Chongro 4-Ga, Chongro-Gu
Seoul 110-124, South Korea
Tel. +82 27 45 61 51
www.mccann.com

Mario Lombardo

Weigertpirouzwolf
Waterloohain 9
22769 Hamburg
Germany
Tel. +49 40 14 32 390
www.weigertpirouzwolf.de

DDB Singapore
226 Outram Road
Singapore 169039
Singapore
Tel. +65 63 23 48 11
www.ddb.com.sg

BBDP Düsseldorf

Jung von Matt
Glashüttenstraße 38
20357 Hamburg
Germany
Tel. +49 40 43 210
www.jvm.de

Saatchi & Saatchi, Mumbai
Sitaram Mills Compound
N.M. Joshi Marg, Delisle Road
400 011 Mumbai, India
Tel. +91 22 23 00 03 01
www.saatchi.com

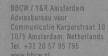

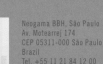

Weigertpirouzwolf
Waterloohain 9
22769 Hamburg
Germany
Tel. +49 40 14 32 390
www.weigertpirouzwolf.de

DDB Buenos Aires
Juncal 1207
C1062ABM Buenos Aires
Argentina
Tel. +54 11 57 77 50 00
www.ddb.com

Leo Burnett, Oslo
Drammensveien 130
Building 4B. Skoyen N-0212
Oslo, Norway
Tel. +47 24 10 39 00
www.leoburnett.no

Bull Calvert Pace
St Andrews Office Park,
Meadowbrook Lane, Bryanston
Johannesburg, South Africa
Tel. +27 11 78 06 100
www.ilbcp.co.za

TBWA / PARIS
Rue de Billancourt 162-164
92103 Boulogne-Billancourt
BP 411, France
Tel. +33 14 90 97 010
www.tbwa-france.com

Springer & Jacoby Werbung
Poststraße 14-16
20354 Hamburg
Germany
Tel. +49 40 35 60 30
www.sj.com

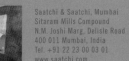

Publicis, Zürich
Theaterstraße 8
8001 Zürich
Switzerland
Tel. +41 44 26 53 111
www.publicis.ch

Young & Rubicam, São Paulo
Rua General Furtado do
Nascimento 9, CEP 05465-
070 São Paulo, Brazil
Tel. +55 11 30 26 44 00
www.y&r.com

Saatchi & Saatchi, Mumbai
Sitaram Mills Compound
N.M. Joshi Marg, Delisle Road
400 011 Mumbai, India
Tel. +91 22 23 00 03 01
www.saatchi.com

F Nazca Saatchi & Saatchi
Av. República do Libano 253
Ibirapuera
04501-000 São Paulo, Brazil
Tel. +55 11 30 59 48 00
www.fnazca.com.br

Saatchi & Saatchi, London
80 Charlotte Street
London W1A 1AQ
United Kingdom
Tel. +44 20 7636 5060
www.saatchi.com

TBWA / BR
Rua Butantã 518 6° andar
05424-000 São Paulo
Brazil
Tel. +55 11 3038-0500
www.tbwa.com.br

Bold / TBWA Oslo
Skoyen, Reklamebyra A5
Karenslyst Allè 18D
0213 Oslo, Norway
Tel. +47 22 12 99 99
www.tbwa.no

Kolle Rebbe
Werbeagentur GmbH
Dienerreihe 2
20457 Hamburg, Germany
Tel. +49 40 32 54 230
www.kolle-rebbe.de

McCann Erickson, Singapore
360 Orchard Road #03-00
238869 Singapore
Singapore
Tel. +65 67 37 99 11
www.mccann.com

Springer & Jacoby Werbung
Poststraße 14-16
20354 Hamburg
Germany
Tel. +49 40 35 60 30
www.sj.com

Amsterdam Advertising
De Oude Molen 1
1184 VW Oudekerk a/d Amstel
Netherlands
Tel. +30 20 63 60 595
www.amsterdamadvertising.nl

Tandem Campmany Guasch/
DDB Barcelona
Enrique Granados 86-88
08008 Barcelona, Spain
Tel. +34 93 22 83 400
www.ddb.com

D'Arcy
Cronenburg 2
1081 GN 1008 BE Amsterdam
Netherlands
Tel. +31 30 50 46 161
www.darcy.nl

PICTURE CREDITS

p. 4: Photo: Thomas Mayer p. 7: Photo: Tobias Prasse p. 206-1: Picture: http://www.kepler.nasa.gov/johannes (08/2005) p. 206-2: Manfred Ritter, *Wahrnehmung und visuelles System*, Spektrum der Wissenschaft Verlagsgesellschaft, Heidelberg, 1987 p. 207-1: E. Bruce Goldstein, *Sensation and Perception*, Wadsworth-Thomson Learning, Pacific Grove, CA, 2002 p. 207-2: Conrad George Mueller, *Light and Vision*, Time, Inc., New York, 1966 p. 207-3: Jacques Ninio, *Macht Schwarz schlank?*, Gustav Kiepenheuer Verlag, Berlin, 1999 p. 208-1: Photo: Arek Godlewski p. 208-2: Photo: stock.xchng p. 208-3: Photo: PixelQuelle.de p. 209-1: Donald D. Hoffman, *Visual Intelligence*, W. W. Norton & Company, New York, 1998 p. 209-2: Photos: stock.xchng p. 210-1: Irvin Rock, *Perception*, Scientific American Library, New York, 1984 p. 210-2: Photo: http://www.institut-lumiere.org/english/lumiere/sfilms.html (08/2005) p. 211-1: Photo: http://sunside.berkeley.edu/uchistory (08/2005) p. 211-2: Pictures: http://online-media.uni-marburg.de/kunstgeschichte/sds (07/2005) p. 212-1: Donald D. Hoffman, *Visual Intelligence*, W. W. Norton & Company, New York, 1998 p. 212-2: Picture: http://www.game.csie.ndhu.edu.tw/works/SIRDS/SIRDS.htm (07/2005) p. 213-1: Photo: Nicole Adelt p. 213-2: R. Goscinny and A. Uderzo, *Asterix* Vol. 22, *The Great Crossing*, Orion, London, 2004 p. 213-3: Photo: Volkmar Otto (http://www.ratiopharm.de) (09/2005) p. 215: Nils Jockel and Werner Lippert, *Und läuft und läuft und läuft: Käfer, New Beatle und die perfekte Form*, Prestel, Munich, 1999 p. 216-1: Martin Riehl, *Vers une Architecture: Das moderne Bauprogramm des Le Corbusier*, scaneg, Munich, 1992 p. 216-2: Picture: http://zeichnen.gemutlichkeit.de/html/Zeichnen_Grundlagen/Perspektive/nichtlineare_Perspektiven/bedeutungsperspektive.htm (08/2005) p. 217-1: Picture: http://www.mathe.tu-freiberg.de/~hebisch/cafe/duerer/laute.html (08/2005) p. 217-2: Bernhard Schütz, *Die kirchliche Barockarchitektur in Bayern und Oberschwaben 1580-1780*, Hirmer Verlag, Munich, 2000 p. 217-3: Picture: http://www.atara.net/magritte/60s/blank-check.html (07/2005) p. 218-1: Alfons Schilling, *Ich/Auge/Welt: The Art Of Vision*, Springer-Verlag, Vienna, 1977 p. 218-2: Alfons Schilling, *Ich/Auge/Welt: The Art Of Vision*, Springer-Verlag, Vienna, 1977 p. 218-3: Alfons Schilling, *Ich/Auge/Welt: The Art Of Vision*, Springer-Verlag, Vienna, 1977 p. 218-4: Peter Pakesch, *Einbildung: Das Wahrnehmen in der Kunst*, Walther König, Cologne, 2004 p. 219-1-3: Peter Pakesch, *Einbildung: Das Wahrnehmen in der Kunst*, Walther König, Cologne, 2004 p. 219-4: Bruno Ernst, *The Eye Beguiled*, Taschen, Cologne, 1998 p. 220-1: Moritz Zwimpfer, *2D Visuelle Wahrnehmung*, Verlag Niggli, Sulgen, 1994 p. 220-2: Conrad George Mueller, *Light and Vision*, Time, Inc., New York, 1966 p. 222-1: Donald D. Hoffman, *Visual Intelligence*, W. W. Norton & Company, New York, 1998 p. 222-2: Bruno Ernst, *The Eye Beguiled*, Taschen, Cologne, 1998 p. 222-3: Conrad George Mueller, *Light and Vision*, Time, Inc., New York, 1966 p. 222-4: Irvin Rock, *Perception*, Scientific American Library, New York, 1984 p. 223-1: William Turton, *A Conchological Dictionary of the British Islands*, London, 1819 p. 223-2: Donald D. Hoffman, *Visual Intelligence*, W. W. Norton & Company, New York, 1998 p. 223-3: Peter Jenny, *Quer/Aug/Ein – Kreativität als Prozess: Eine Schulung anschaulichen Denkens*, Verlag der Fachvereine, Zurich, 1989 p. 223-4: Irvin Rock, *Perception*, Scientific American Library, New York, 1984 p. 223-5: Roger N. Shepard, *Mind Sights: Original Visual Illusions, Ambiguities, and other Anomalies*, W.H. Freeman and Co., New York, 1990 p. 224-1: Picture: http://www.worldofescher.com/gallery/A30L.html (08/2005) p. 224-2: Roger N. Shepard, *Mind Sights: Original Visual Illusions, Ambiguities, and other Anomalies*, W.H. Freeman and Co., New York, 1990 p. 224-3: Bruno Ernst, *The Eye Beguiled*, Taschen, Cologne, 1998 p. 224-4: Kyung-Sun Jung, *The Best In World Trademarks: Corporate and Brand Identity*, Millim Publishing, Seoul, 2000 p. 225-1: Bruno Ernst, *The Eye Beguiled*, Taschen, Cologne, 1998 p. 225-2: John P. Frisby, *Seeing: Illusion, Brain And Mind*, Oxford University Press, 1980 p. 225-3: R. Goscinny and A. Uderzo, *Asterix* Vol. 4, *Asterix and the Big Fight*, Orion, London, 2004 p. 225-4 left: Photo: http://www.gettyimages.com p. 225-4 right: Alan Fletcher, *The Art Of Looking Sideways*, Phaidon Press, London, 2001 p. 226: Donald D. Hoffman, *Visual Intelligence*, W. W. Norton & Company, New York, 1998 p. 227: Peter Pakesch, *Einbildung: Das Wahrnehmen in der Kunst*, Walther König, Cologne, 2004 p. 228-1: Alan Fletcher, *The Art Of Looking Sideways*, Phaidon Press, London, 2001 p. 228-2: Peter Pakesch, *Einbildung: Das Wahrnehmen in der Kunst*, Walther König, Cologne, 2004 p. 228-3: Bruno Ernst, *The Eye Beguiled*, Taschen, Cologne, 1998 p. 228-4: John P. Frisby, *Seeing: Illusion, Brain And Mind*, Oxford University Press, Oxford, 1980 p. 229-1: Miriam Milman, *Trompe-L'Oeil Painting*, Editions d'Art Albert Skira, Geneva, 1982 p. 229-2: Bruno Ernst, *The Eye Beguiled*, Taschen, Cologne, 1998 p. 229-3: Miriam Milman, *Trompe-L'Oeil Painting*, Editions d'Art Albert Skira, Geneva, 1982 p. 230-1: Donald D. Hoffman, *Visual Intelligence*, W.W. Norton & Company, New York, 1998 p. 230-2: Roger N. Shepard, *Mind Sights: Original Visual Illusions, Ambiguities, and other Anomalies*, W.H. Freeman and Co., New York, 1990 p. 230-3: Bruno Ernst, *The Eye Beguiled*, Taschen, Cologne, 1998 p. 231-1: Bruno Ernst, *The Eye Beguiled*, Taschen, Cologne, 1998 p. 231-2: Moritz Zwimpfer, *2D Visuelle Wahrnehmung*, Verlag Niggli, Sulgen, 1994 p. 231-3-4: Bruno Ernst, *The Eye Beguiled*, Taschen, Cologne, 1998 p. 232-5: from *Way of the Dragon*, Concord Productions, 1972 p. 233: Alan Fletcher, *The Art Of Looking Sideways*, Phaidon Press, London, 2001 p. 234-1: Conrad George Mueller, *Light and Vision*, Time, Inc., New York, 1966 p. 234-2: Conrad George Mueller, *Light and Vision*, Time, Inc., New York, 1966 p. 234-3: Bruno

The solution to the Dallenbach picture on page 222.

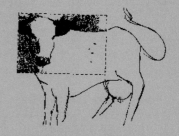

Ernst, *The Eye Beguiled*, Taschen, Cologne, 1998 p. 235: Conrad George Mueller, *Light and Vision*, Time, Inc., New York, 1966 p. 236-1: Jacques Ninio, *Macht Schwarz schlank?*, Gustav Kiepenheuer Verlag, Berlin, 1999 p. 236-2: Conrad George Mueller, *Light and Vision*, Time, Inc., New York, 1966 p. 237: Photo: Felix Dobbert p. 238-1-2: Jacques Ninio, *Macht Schwarz schlank?*, Gustav Kiepenheuer Verlag, Berlin, 1999 p. 238-3: Alan Fletcher, *The Art Of Looking Sideways*, Phaidon Press, London, 2001 p. 238-4: Irvin Rock, *Perception*, Scientific American Library, New York, 1984 p. 239-1: Irvin Rock, *Perception*, Scientific American Library, New York, 1984 p. 239-2-3: Pictures: http://www.illusionworks.com p. 239-4: Irvin Rock, *Perception*, Scientific American Library, New York, 1984 p. 240: Donald D. Hoffman, *Visual Intelligence*, W. W. Norton & Company, New York, 1998 p. 241: Alan Fletcher, *The Art Of Looking Sideways*, Phaidon Press, London, 2001 p. 242-1: Oliver Meckes, *Der Mikrokosmos*, Gruner und Jahr, Hamburg, 2004 p. 242-2: Photo: http://www.derniko.de/reisen (08/2005) p. 242-3: Vincent Van Gogh, original work, Monte von DuMont, Cologne, 2002 p. 243-1 left: Picture: http://www.artnet.com (07/2005) S.243-1 rechts: Tobias Bungter, Pocket Quiz, Optische Illusionen, Moses Verlag p.243-2: Jürgen W. Braun, *Visuelle Kommunikation*, Walther König, Cologne, 1995 p. 244-1: Irvin Rock, *Perception*, Scientific American Library, New York, 1984 p. 244-2: Alan Fletcher, *The Art Of Looking Sideways*, Phaidon Press, London, 2001 p. 245: Peter Pakesch, *Einbildung: Das Wahrnehmen in der Kunst*, Walther König, Cologne, 2004 p. 246-1: Francois Robert and Jean Robert, *Gesichter*, Gerstenberg Verlag, 2005 p. 246-2: Photos: http://giraudalain.neuf.fr/portraitsdebateaux (08/2005) p. 248-1-2: E. Bruce Goldstein, *Sensation and Perception*, Wadsworth-Thomson Learning, Pacific Grove, CA, 2002 p. 249: Markus Raetz, *Eva*, 1983, courtesy of VG Bildkunst, Bonn p. 250-1-4: Jacques Ninio, *Macht Schwarz schlank?*, Gustav Kiepenheuer Verlag, Berlin, 1999 p. 250-5: Irvin Rock, *Perception*, Scientific American Library, New York, 1984 p. 251-1: Irvin Rock, *Perception*, Scientific American Library, New York, 1984 p. 251-4 left: John P. Frisby, *Seeing: Illusion, Brain And Mind*, Oxford University Press, Oxford, 1980 p. 252-1: David Carson, *The End Of Print*, Vol. 1, Bangert Verlag, Munich, 1995 p. 252-2: Alan Fletcher, *The Art Of Looking Sideways*, Phaidon Press, London, 2001 p. 253: Photo of a replica of the Phaistos Disk, Peter Iven p. 254-1: from http://www.spiritproject.de/orakel/kaffeesatz (07/2005) p. 254-2: Picture: http://www.balloon-painting.de/warhol.htm (05/2005) p. 255: Photo: Uwe Stoklossa p. 256-2: Photo: http://www.ilexikon.com/Farbe.html (07/2005) p. 257: Jacques Ninio, *Macht Schwarz schlank?*, Gustav Kiepenheuer Verlag, Berlin, 1999 p. 258-1: Jacques Ninio, *Macht Schwarz schlank?*, Gustav Kiepenheuer Verlag, Berlin, 1999 p. 258-2: Alfons Schilling, *Ich/Auge/Welt: The Art Of Vision*, Springer-Verlag, Vienna, 1977 p. 258-3: Moritz Zwimpfer, *2D Visuelle Wahrnehmung*, Verlag Niggli, Sulgen, 1994 p. 259-2: Donald D. Hoffman, *Visual Intelligence*, W. W. Norton & Company, New York, 1998 p. 259-3: Jacques Ninio, *Macht Schwarz schlank?*, Gustav Kiepenheuer Verlag, Berlin, 1999 p. 259-4: Photo: Uwe Stoklossa; © VG Bildkunst, Bonn 2006 for the following illustrations: p. 200-1, p. 216-1, p. 217-3, p. 218-4, p. 231-1 right, p. 243-1 left, p. 249

The ads in the first section of this book have been reproduced with the kind permission and co-operation of the agencies that created them. This task was undertaken with the utmost care plus a good deal of detective work. There were particular difficulties with older ads, because a year in the life of an ordinary man seems to be the equivalent of ten years in advertising. Consequently, it is possible that with a five-year-old ad, the client is no longer in business, or the agency has changed hands three times in the interim. And so if it should happen that, in spite of all our efforts, our translations, our countless telephone calls and emails to every country you can think of, and our painstaking study of foreign copyright laws, an ad has nevertheless been reproduced whose copyright-holder feels that he or she has been unfairly treated, then the author humbly begs forgiveness. We shall do our best to find out the circumstances under which such a mishap could have occurred. But at the same time, the author hopes that the offended party will also be pleased to see his or her work included among the finest examples of this art in the world. None of the participating agencies, photographers or models for the ads have received money, complimentary copies or other forms of payment for their support, because otherwise the cost of this book would have been prohibitive. If you should have any questions about it, or if you should wish to make corrections to the picture credits or the index of agents for future editions, then please contact me: stoklossa@blicktricks.de

Uwe Stoklossa
was born in Hesse in 1975. After a few failed applications to film academies, he began a degree in communications design in 1996 at the University of Essen. During his studies, he got to know Professor Thomas Rempen, who in 2004 supervised his dissertation on the subject 'I See Nothing That You Can't See'. He soon found himself working to turn this dissertation into a 'proper' book.

Uwe Stoklossa now works as a freelance copywriter and graphic designer in Duisburg, Düsseldorf and Essen, as well as being an assistant to Professor Rempen at the University of Duisburg-Essen.

www.stoklossa.com
www.blicktricks.de
stoklossa@blicktricks.de

Acknowledgments
If it should occur to any of you to write a book all by yourself, let me tell you with hindsight: You can do it! But right from the start, you should make sure that you get as many nice people as possible to help you.

That's how it was with this book. And since this book would probably never have been finished without these people, I would like to like to offer them all my heartfelt thanks.

Thanks, then, to my parents and siblings for everything, a publishing house with thoroughly friendly and efficient people in all departments and a truly wonderful couple at its head, a professor blessed with knowledge, patience, commitment, time, wit and useful contacts, not to mention a very fine office, my thesis proofreader Prof. Claudius Lazzeroni. the Kaiserberg Communication Agency in Duisburg, and my hard-working helpers who kept saving my designer's life when I could no longer cope on my own: Christine Bernard (www.buero-bernard.de), Peter Iven, Carla Zockoll (www.buero-c.de), Ava Bahman, Merle Stuntebeck, Sonja Kleffner, Björn Wieland, Gerolf Reichenthaler (www.riegelreich.de), Zorah-Mari Bauer. Thanks also to Pit Schulz, the GGK Advertising Agency in Zürich and their AD Bruno Züttel, Christiane Gillissen of ADC for giving me access to the archives, Sonja Hohenthanner of Lürzer GmbH for her help and for also giving me access to the archives, the very helpful team at the Kunsthaus in Graz, my honorary interpreters – the Straszewski family, Angelika Kaulbach (French), Ligia Fonseca (Portuguese), Anna Rost, Javier Suarez Argueta, and Katja Werthmann (Spanish) – my favourite photographers, Tobias Prasse (www.tobiasprasse.com) and Felix Dobbert (www.felix-dobbert.de), Steffi Toloszycki for financial and moral support, my bankers Stuntebeck and Bernard, Gunter Liermann for the many old Lürzer books, Dorothea Frink for providing the right keys at the right time, Maze Café/Restaurant (www.maze-lounge.de), Weber, Werner, Reith, Marx for many outstanding culinary occasions, and Jörn Burger, Frank Haus, Romeu Valadares, Andreas Hahn and Meike Lenzen for being everything that friends are supposed to be.

Translated from the German *Blicktricks: Anleitung zur Visuelle Verführung*
by David H. Wilson

First published in the United Kingdom in 2007 by
Thames & Hudson Ltd, 181A High Holborn, London WC1V 7QX

www.thamesandhudson.com

First published in 2007 in hardcover in the United States of America by
Thames & Hudson Inc., 500 Fifth Avenue, New York, New York 10110

thamesandhudsonusa.com

First paperback edition 2010

British Library Cataloguing-in-Publication Data
A catalogue record for this book is available from the British Library

Library of Congress Catalog Card Number 2006906108

ISBN: 978-0-500-28909-9

Printed in Singapore